Made
Well

Books by Jenny Simmons

The Road to Becoming
Made Well

Made Well

finding WHOLENESS in
the EVERYDAY SACRED Moments

JENNY SIMMONS

BakerBooks

a division of Baker Publishing Group
Grand Rapids, Michigan

Published by Baker Books
a division of Baker Publishing Group
P.O. Box 6287, Grand Rapids, MI 49516-6287
www.bakerbooks.com

Printed in the United States of America

Library of Congress Cataloging-in-Publication Data
Names: Simmons, Jenny, author.
Title: Made well : finding wholeness in the everyday sacred moments / Jenny
    Simmons.
Description: Grand Rapids : Baker Books, 2016. | Includes bibliographical
    references.
Identifiers: LCCN 2016017284 | ISBN 9780801018909 (pbk.)
Subjects: LCSH: Spiritual healing. | Healing—Religious aspects—Christianity.
Classification: LCC BT732.5 .S537 2016 | DDC 248.8/6—dc23
LC record available at https://lccn.loc.gov/2016017284

Some names and details have been changed to protect the pri-
vacy of the individuals involved.

16   17   18   19   20   21   22   7   6   5   4   3   2   1

"Healing is a long, hard road. I am grateful for Jenny's writing that acknowledges this truth while also being steeped in the nearness of Jesus. Life-giving hope whispers from these pages."

from the foreword by **Margaret Feinberg**,
author of *Fight Back with Joy*

"Jenny Simmons's *Made Well* simply gushes grace. Alternately heart-breaking, funny, raw—but most of all unbearably human. I can't recall reading a more authentic book on spirituality. Simmons's ease in her own skin and command of her craft combine to make a book that is as substantive as it is tender. Real-life, hard-edged truth crackles on every page. *Made Well* is a work of tremendous soul, a book that, like its author, sings. I can't recommend it highly enough."

Jonathan Martin, author of *How to Survive a Shipwreck*
and *Prototype*

"Carrying her words as only a poet would, Jenny Simmons stands at the mic in her emotional skivvies and sings the miracle of belief, where if we dare to wake up, we'll see God's love and power have never been clearer. *Made Well* offers the courage to lean into the ordinary—friendship, therapy, laundry, tacos—and see it as wholly belonging to our Father. Often the sea is parted through the daily crumbs of a life spent longing. Emmanuel finds us here, in yesterday's yoga pants with pancake batter in our hair, and, as Jenny says, 'transforms the holes.' This book is a necessary reminder that there is no such thing as ordinary healing."

Shannan Martin, author of *Falling Free*

"What happens when the pain gets worse, the days get harder, and healing doesn't come the way we expected? Oftentimes faith is re-duced to a try-harder and do-more mantra we chant when the world seems dark or painful or so full of death and brokenness that we can't imagine hope would survive. This book is for those of us who feel a little too broken, a little too messy, a little too unwell. Sometimes in the disappointments, the questions, the crushing ache, we find God was there with us all along. Jenny Simmons's redemptive story offers a simple invitation to look at wholeness and healing as something that is intrinsically linked to the sacred ordinary, a work God is already doing in the places we least expect it."

Alia Joy, (in)courage writer

"I'm a champion for helping people find a redemptive purpose in their pain and for helping them take ownership of the broken things within us and around us. Jenny's authentic words will amplify hope that being made well is possible—in more ways than you might have realized—and it's happening all around you every day. You *can* find wholeness in the ordinary sacred moments, if you will take time to notice. This book will show you the way and remind you of God's abiding love."

Mike Foster, author, pastor, and founder of People of the Second Chance

"When I was growing up and I skinned my knee, my mom would kiss it and put a Band-Aid on it. Unfortunately, this is the same approach I continued to use every time I would get wounded in life. What Jenny has done in *Made Well* is not shame the reader into acknowledging that healing takes more than a kiss and a Band-Aid, but she has guided the reader into a safe space where healing can actually happen. This book is a gift to those in need of healing."

Carlos Whittaker, author, speaker, and entrepreneur

"Two things about *Made Well* deeply resonate with me: vulnerability and hope. Jenny Simmons writes with disarming honesty about the path toward healing in the midst of suffering. We often pray for God to fix our broken situations and heal our bodies, but what happens when those prayers aren't answered in the ways we thought they would be? This book explores the surprising and unexpected ways God faithfully meets us in our brokenness and leads us toward wholeness. Laced with humorous confession and abounding grace, this story looks a lot like hope. If you need a companion on the road to being made well, start here. This book is a balm for the weary."

Rev. Eugene Cho, pastor, humanitarian, and author of *Overrated*

"The first time I met Jenny Simmons I was drawn to her honesty and self-awareness. In a world where so many of us struggle to put ourselves out there, Jenny is a breath of fresh air. She's not afraid to share the hard parts of her life and her journey of healing. For anyone who hasn't experienced an overnight miracle, this book is for you. Being made well doesn't come without a cost, but these brave stories will breathe hope into your journey and inspire you to keep pressing forward."

Lindsey Nobles, COO and chief strategist of IF:Gathering

"Jenny is my kindred spirit. The type of kindred spirit who keeps you close to the truth of who God is whether you're in the depths of inconsolable grief or basking in a glorious victory. In her book *Made Well: Finding Wholeness in the Everyday Sacred Moments*, she will become your kindred too. Through her honesty and relentless pursuit of healing, Jenny will challenge and inspire you to find freedom through a soul made well."

Trisha Davis, cofounder of RefineUs Ministries and Hope City Church and coauthor of *Beyond Ordinary*

This book is for my brave sister Sarah. And Karissa, Stephanie, Karen, Jill, and Amanda. And for every person who daily fights to be made well. You have faced devastating trauma, impossible odds, and unspeakable evil, but you keep fighting for healing. Yours is holy work. Thank you for teaching us what it looks like to be made well.

And for Maggie and Ellen, whose laughter I never knew. You taught me most about being made well.

Contents

Contents

Foreword

We walk among the fellowship of the afflicted now. Like the tearing of bread at communion, you can put two halves back together again, but life will never be the same.

We speak a different language regarding pain and loss that those who haven't experienced deep suffering don't always understand. You must be plunged in horror. A barren desert we would never choose. Wild beasts we'd only dream of facing in our worst nightmares. But if Christ is at the center, a new life will be poured out. In God's kingdom, weak is the new strong, poor is the new rich, broken is the new whole.

I wrote these words to my friend Jenny Simmons while fighting the hardest battle of my life. She was on the heels of deep grief as well, having buried multiple members of her family in a few months.

We were both thrust into horrendous, life-altering journeys and had to decide whether we would fight back with joy or give up hope in the midst of unending pain. Through grace, we both found God's merciful providence in the recesses of our suffering. Evidence of God's presence leaked everywhere.

Divine timing remains a mystery. A gift. Sometimes it feels like a double-edged sword. The horror and heartbreak. The healing and wholeness. Tears and joy commingle in the most mysterious ways. Jenny knows these paradoxes well and does what every good storyteller does best: she gives us permission to lean into both.

Through this collection of vulnerable and hopeful stories, she teaches us that wholeness waits along rugged roads we never thought we would travel. Speaking to those walking through dark seasons of pain, Jenny offers a healing balm that isn't found by traipsing the world but in the simplicity of sacred moments among ordinary lives.

Healing is a long, hard road. I am grateful for Jenny's writing that acknowledges this truth while also being steeped in the nearness of Jesus. Life-giving hope whispers from these pages.

The humorous and poetic words of this book invite you to make the journey of healing with a host of friends by your side: Christian therapists, psychiatrists, pastors, nurses, friends, spouses, churches, hiking trails, nature, food, family, and God.

The march of the afflicted *is* long. But Jenny gives us permission to seek beauty and freedom as we are made well by the Healer. And I give you permission to fight back with joy.

—Margaret Feinberg, author of *Fight Back with Joy*

In the Beginning

*I*n the beginning, you were made well.

Designed with divine imagination, shaped by sacred hands, and crafted by the Curator of creation.

You and I were called good. We were *already* enough. It was the original plan.

Fearfully and wonderfully made in the very image of God—we mirrored our Creator. Sally Lloyd Jones says it beautifully in *The Jesus Storybook Bible*: "When God saw them he was like a new dad. 'You look like me,' he said. 'You're the most beautiful thing I've ever made!' God loved them with all of his heart. And they were lovely because he loved them."[1]

Our heritage was God hovering over the nothingness, creating everything. Our destiny was divine companionship. We were created perfect and blameless. There was no shame, envy, pain, tears, doubt, fear . . . death. There was no dying. Eden was the only utopia this world has ever known. In it, a holy synergy existed between nature, weather, animals, land, humans, and the Curator himself. God took long walks in the cool of the evening with His beloved children. Everything was as it should be.

But there was one who hated God and burned with jealousy. His spirit entered the world and planted deception in the hearts of God's children. The fear of missing out crept into humanity. Doubt ran wild. Were we really loved? Eve's heart became obsessed. What if God was keeping something from her? Was there more to Eden than she knew? Lack of knowledge ate away at her soul. There *was* that one rule God had given. The only rule. Don't eat from the tree of the knowledge of good and evil—doing so would open her eyes to that which she was never meant to see. She had everything she needed, but it was too late. Eve was tormented and could not resist the voice that told her she was entitled to have what the tree offered. Adam followed closely behind. And with one bite, the gap between the now and the not yet was born.

Death stormed in. Fear followed. Pain and shame came close behind.

It was the end of perfect companionship between God and His children.

And the beginning of a once holy people learning to live with their holes.

Separation from our original identity, our true home, and the God who walked among His children entered the picture. The story changed. We were no longer in perfect union with our Creator or His creation, so God set His eyes to an unrelenting rescue mission. A rescue that will one day culminate in all things being made well forever. A place where children will once again enjoy long walks in the cool of the evening in God's presence. But until then . . .

We live in the heartbreaking tension of the now and the not yet.

We long for wholeness.

We look for the way back to our true home.

Blackbird

My Mamaw died in April as they were painting her toenails. It didn't matter if she was ever getting out of that bed again or not; there would be nail polish and perfectly primped hair. From my dad's mom, I get my beauty standards, Southern hospitality, and propensity to cook copious amounts of food for family gatherings. She had three refrigerators and a deep freezer in her modest home, which seems like a completely acceptable family tradition for me to carry on. The last time we saw one another, I helped move her from her portable toilet seat back to the bed she was confined to. She looked at me and giggled. I had never seen Mamaw giggle like that.

"Now, who are you?" she said playfully, like a child.

"Mamaw, it's me, Jenny, your oldest grandchild. You know me."

"Oh, that's right, that's right." She patted my hand with a far-off look—a body, but not a mind. I kept the tears inside until

I left the room, and then they didn't stop for two days. Three months later, my mom's dad was next.

I know you shouldn't have a favorite grandparent, but I can't help it. Grandpa was mine. Maybe because my momma loved him so much or because he taught me how to tell a good story. Definitely because of the way he always said, "I love you, baby," with that thick, South Dakotan accent of his. He was young. Too young to die. And although he was sick, no one knew it was going to be his last night. Just before they took him off life support, my mom told him it was going to be okay and he shook his head no. Not this time. It took four hours after they removed life support for him to pass from this world to the next. His daughters held his hands and held their breath. I held my cell phone high above the water and watched the texts come across the screen while in the swimming pool with my daughter, Annie, and the neighborhood kids. It was the worst play-by-play of my life. A part of my heart is still on the bottom of that pool. Dying feels so long.

After Grandpa's funeral my mom said, "Enough with dying, on to living!" We turned our attention to my baby sister Sarah, who had made peace with the fact that her one biological daughter would probably be the only child she would ever be able to give birth to. After three miscarriages and a complicated pregnancy with their daughter Abigail, she and her husband, Ray, began to pursue adoption. It had always been their dream to adopt, it was just coming sooner than they imagined. After all the paperwork was complete and they were waiting to be placed with a child, they found out they were pregnant. *With twins.*

My family's shock quickly turned to excitement. Twins?! We weren't sure of their gender yet, but my two sisters and I have proven ourselves incapable of creating boys, so we knew—two beautiful baby girls were on their way. Our family began to dream about what life would be like with twin cousins, nieces, granddaughters, and daughters. Their living eased the dying.

Sarah bought an at-home fetal heart-rate monitor, and we gathered around to listen to the pitter-patter of their tiny racing hearts. But three weeks after Grandpa's funeral, Sarah was diagnosed with a rare condition called twin-to-twin transfusion syndrome that occurs in a very small percentage of identical twins. The doctors said that without treatment, the condition would prove fatal for at least one of the babies, and they began to discuss Sarah's options, including a highly specialized surgery that used a laser to split the conjoined blood vessels in their shared placenta. Our excitement turned to fear. None of us had ever heard of this condition or procedure, but it was the only hope they gave my sister, so we set our sights on surgery.

Four days after the first shocking diagnosis, we received another one. Sarah called my mom to tell her that her water had broken and she was being rushed to the hospital. She was seventeen weeks pregnant. Although the babies were given little to no chance of survival, the doctors began aggressively treating Sarah with antibiotics to ward off infection with the ultimate hopes of keeping the girls in utero. After nine days of treatment and no improvement, the doctors said it was hopeless. It would only be a matter of days before the girls would die. Sarah asked to be sent home to wait for labor to begin, and her medical team agreed to the plan.

But labor never began.

For six agonizing weeks the girls lived. They grew strong, hiccuped inside their momma's ever-widening belly, and kept us on our knees praying for a miracle. We were told if they could hang on, there might be a chance of survival. For weeks we lived between life and death, never knowing what the outcome would be. Everything in me begged, pleaded, and bartered for a miracle. I must have cried a million tears and muttered just as many prayers. "Oh, Jesus, you can save these babies. So do it. Save these babies." I longed for a miracle, and yet I knew enough about the way this broken world works that I also wanted to protect myself. I just couldn't figure out how.

Never knowing what news might be on the other end when the phone rang took its toll. Each time someone called, my heart rate skyrocketed, my stomach knotted up, my entire body braced for the news. But it was only Walgreens calling to tell me my prescription was ready or a friend calling to see if we needed anything. Living between life and death was a kind of exhausting hell I did not know was possible.

Sarah and Ray never gave up hope. They poured more love into those little girls than some kids receive in a lifetime—constantly reading, singing, and praying over them, all the while telling them how loved they were. They carefully chose the girls' names and took family photos with two tiny rocking chairs to represent the girls growing inside. Sarah walked through each new day with a kind of superhuman faith. She watched the rise and fall of her stomach as her daughters played and grew, and she believed for their future. The specialists said they had never seen anything like it—even *they* thought we were experiencing a miracle. And we were. Every second they lived inside of her was a miracle.

But on the morning of October 2nd, Sarah woke up at death's door. When her water broke, it left her highly susceptible to infection, and that morning her body finally succumbed to the possibility. She was riddled with infection. I caught the first flight out of Nashville and was in her hospital room by 1:00 p.m. Her situation was perilous. She was so sick she could not be operated on, nor could she have any medicine for the pain. A C-section was not an option, as it would kill her. She had to give birth to these girls naturally, knowing that at twenty-three weeks, without the amniotic fluid in utero they needed to practice breathing, they would die as soon as they came into this world.

The doctors apologized often, then gently reminded those of us in the room that someone was going to die that day, and they didn't want it to be Sarah. She had to push. She had to give birth. With each new contraction she apologized to the girls—giving birth to them meant their death.

Maggie Jane and Ellen Olivia were born at 7:30 p.m. on October 2, 2014. They died moments later in my sister's arms.

The funeral home came the next day. Until then, the girls lay on Sarah's chest like little dolls. Ellen had the same button nose as my daughter, Annie. I stared at their faces, ran my fingers over their tiny toes, and wondered how I would ever leave that hospital. The pain was too great and I was too broken.

The miracle we prayed for hadn't happened.

Lucky Lady in the House!

On October 16th, five days after my nieces' funeral, I woke up and told Ryan I was probably *not* a good candidate for a date that night. Perhaps he could ask a friend to go see Paul McCartney with him instead of me.

I had come home from Maggie and Ellen's funeral stunned and unsure of how to step back into normal life. The better part of the year had been spent on dying, and it felt daunting to relearn how to start living. I was walking into four weekends in a row of concert performances and leading worship at women's conferences, and I needed to pull myself together so I could get back to work. But I was pretty sure that was not going to happen in a sold-out arena with frenzied Beatles fans. I *so* wasn't ready to be around humanity yet. But Ryan persisted. We only had to stay for a few songs and then we could leave, he said. And he really wanted to share the moment with me, not somebody else. I had known that much since we started dating fifteen years ago—seeing Paul McCartney in concert was one of the few things on the man's bucket list. Plus, music would be good for my soul, he assured me; it might even make me well. So, begrudgingly, I went.

We fought about everything. Where to park, which entrance to use, what food line to stand in. There was a new taqueria in the arena, and I took this as a sign of God's abundant love for me. Mexican food is a sure way to my heart. But Ryan insisted that one could not eat tacos at such a venue, only shriveled hot dogs or stale nachos. We bickered like babies over tacos and hot dogs. I was angry with myself for leaving the house long before we even found our seats. And they were *awful* seats. The only tickets I could afford six months before, when I bought the surprise Father's Day gift, were at the tippy-top of the arena. And by tippy-top, I mean three rows from the very back wall of the cement building.

We finally made it to the upper level of the arena and took a peek at our seats before deciding on what food to get in the lobby. The seats felt like they were a thousand miles away from the stage—we might as well watch from home, I angrily thought. It was cold and dark up there, like the morning of the funeral, when it was so frigid outside the funeral home offered us blankets to wrap up in as we sat under the green tent and listened to the words of the preacher and the pitter-patter of rain falling on the tiny casket.

I tried to push back the memory and, with it, the tears. "I will not cry. I will not cry," I repeated while scolding myself for having left the house.

We turned around to go get food in the lobby. And that's when she walked directly up to Ryan and me and said, "Hey! Are you guys excited about the concert tonight?!"

She was a complete stranger in the midst of thousands of people making their way into the upper-level seats, and we had no idea why she was talking to us. I panicked and wondered if I should know her from somewhere. But I was sure I'd never seen her, and her bubbly energy was driving me crazy. She was *way* too happy for my current state.

Ryan politely smiled. "Yeah. Can't wait. How about you?"

She disregarded his obligatory question. "Are you big fans?" she asked.

"Yeah, huge fans," Ryan said as he tried to walk past her.

"How big?" she questioned and flashed her hands in front of her face like jazz hands.

I was so annoyed. Pretty-happy people are the worst when you are grieving. *What's wrong with this girl?* I thought. *Leave us alone. I'm about four teardrops away from triggering a monsoon, and I do not have the emotional fortitude to endure talking to pretty-happy people like you.*

Ryan began to rattle off the names of Paul's albums, the Beatles' albums, and song titles. I continued to talk badly about the girl in my head. Then she looked me straight in the eyes and said, "Great. You looked like the right couple. Take this and go fast—these are much better seats. Floor seats! But seriously—you have to get down there fast!"

She thrust a white envelope into my hands and disappeared. We were stunned. It happened so quickly we didn't have time to process. We took the envelope without opening it and made our way against the push of people, getting to the floor in a matter of minutes. I felt my heart racing with adrenaline and shock. Floor seats to the sold-out Paul McCartney show—was this really happening?

Ryan told me to go find our new spot while he headed to get hot dogs. I let the tacos go. I found an older man who was serving as an usher and handed him the unopened envelope. "Hi. I just got these tickets. Sorry, I haven't even opened them yet."

He pulled the tickets from the envelope, and a huge smile broke out from ear to ear. "So *you* are the lucky lady in the house tonight!" he exclaimed.

And with those ten words my heart stood still and the tears came. The dam I had so carefully constructed gave way, and the reservoir flowed freely down my face. This poor man probably thought I was insane. I looked at him and shook my head. *No, I am not the lucky lady in the house tonight*, I thought. I didn't need to tell him about the pain I was walking through—he was just doing his job. He didn't need to know what I had seen five days earlier. How my dad had carried Maggie and Ellen's tiny casket into the rain and knelt down on a green tarp and lowered his grandbabies into the wet ground. No one needed to know that pain. No one should have to see that.

I apologized for the tears and simply said, "It's been a hard week."

"Well, tonight is your lucky night then, honey! Before our biggest shows they send an intern upstairs to give away a pair of front-row seats. Front row! Out of fifteen thousand people, they picked you. I'd say that's an awfully lucky night." He smiled a deep, knowing smile and patted my back. "Let's get you up front."

His words rang in my head. *They picked you.*

God whispered, *I picked you.*

Take These Broken Wings

Some people are made well through running, baking, painting, hiking, hammering through an old wall, or driving in no particular direction with no particular destination. I listen to music. It carries me away and reminds me of what is beautiful and constant. It heals me. Music has been my dearest and most faithful companion.

As I sat in the front row waiting for the show to begin, I stood up and turned around to take in the thousands of people behind me and couldn't keep the tears from streaming down my face. I knew in that moment that this was the most extravagant way God could reach down from heaven, scoop me up, and begin to bandage my wounds. Sitting so close I could hear Paul McCartney's foot stomping out the tempo for each new song, I let the melodies of some of the world's most famous songs wash over me like medicine. "Blackbird," "Here Comes the Sun," "All You Need Is Love," "Hey Jude," "Yesterday," and "Let It Be"—for three and a half hours, he sang his words of wisdom over me. *Let it be.* As the song "Blackbird" started and the stage began to rise, Paul McCartney uttered the words my heart desperately needed to hear—that I could take these broken wings and learn to fly. It became my prayer. *God, show me how to fly again.*

Something in me began to mend in those moments. The way a Band-Aid placed on a wide-open cut immediately begins to bring the wound together and bind it, the songs began to bind broken bits back together in my heart. It seemed God Himself had orchestrated an evening for me in a way that only the Great Physician could. It wasn't the miracle I prayed for, but it was a miracle all the same. Emmanuel showing up in the hardest moments, holding my hand. And I realized that night that my being made well through music was His divine hand of healing.

Healing happens all the time, even if a cure doesn't. I am invited to be made well even when the broken things don't get put perfectly back together. Healing happens. It can happen after the divorce, after the funeral, after the abuse, after the lost job, after the miracle you prayed for doesn't come to pass. After you bury the babies. Even in those spaces, wholeness can come again and you can be made well.

I've often wondered what happens to a person when the miracle they pray for doesn't come to pass. Now I know. I remember every time I hear the song "Blackbird." Healing happens—if you let it.

Half-Baked Miracles

My husband and I started a band during college and spent the following decade crisscrossing the country on tour with our bandmates. We played everywhere from tiny coffee shops to state fairs to arenas, and one year we had the honor of performing at the prestigious Montana Music Festival. I should have known it was going to be a special night when the college kid next to me on the airplane said, "Where are you going?" and my answer to him was followed by a long, quizzical pause. He finally ventured to say, "I've lived in Montana for twenty-four years and never heard of that town *or* that festival. Are you sure you're headed to the right state?" He laughed and looked at me like I hadn't read a map; his eyes assured me the town did not exist.

After an exhausting ten-hour travel day that included three states, two plane rides, a rental car, and an hour-long drive, we arrived in the tiny blip of a town and met the promoter. She promptly apologized and informed us she wouldn't be able to pay our contracted fee or reimburse the two thousand dollars we had already spent on airline tickets to get there. We were automatically seven thousand dollars in the hole. As it turns out, the festival was more of an idea in her head than an actual event. It was attended by twenty-seven people in the middle of a muddy pasture during the worst rain- and windstorm I've ever seen in my life.

As we waited to play for twenty-seven people, the rainstorm with tsunami-like winds descended and furiously swept over the land. I found myself running for cover, but since we were literally in a field, the options were limited. My bandmates and husband opted to run clear across the pasture and take cover in an old, dingy RV. But I was wearing high heels, so I ran inside the first tent I saw. And that's where I met Jimmy the worm farmer.

Years ago, Jimmy noticed the side of his garden that was over-run with worms always exploded in growth, and he deduced that it *must* be on account of the worms' poop. He collected the worms, waited for them to poop, and then sent that poop off to some sort of science lab where they can tell you what kind of vitamins and minerals show up in your animals' excrement. This is a real thing. The lab results came back, and Jimmy realized he had pure gold on his hands. Pure. Gold. There was more goodness in one Dixie cup of worm-poop manure than an entire bag of store-bought fertilizer.

So Jimmy invested in worms. Millions of them. Now he collects their poop and sells it in small quantities to local farmers.

And of course he's at the festival to sell worm poop, because that is what happens at *every proper music festival*. There is a man who looks like a nomadic goat shepherd, who pitches a tent and sits all day long with his hands soaked in worm poop. *Of course there is.* And I am in his tent, waiting out a rainstorm, hearing about the revolution of worm poop, when he says in his long, drawn-out country accent, "Feel of it, Jenny. You just feel of it. It's softer than silk! Smell it!"

I tried to exaggerate the size of my eyes as I said, "Wow, that does look soft, Jimmy!" But that didn't cut it. He wanted me to touch it.

"No, really, just run your fingers through it." He picked up a mound of silky poop in his dry, cracked hands and poured it all over mine. Then he took my hands and practically shoved them, elbows deep, into a burlap potato sack full of worm poop. I was horrified.

I looked out over a vast expanse of land and thought, *What in the world am I doing with my life?* I was exhausted from the travel and angry with the lady who'd deceived us and not honored the contract. Nothing was going the way it was supposed to, and yet right there in the middle of it was Jimmy and his completely unbridled worm joy. And I started to laugh out loud in that tent as the rain pounded down from the skies. Uncontrollable laughter. Because what else can you do in a moment like that? When you are trapped in a tent, in a rainstorm, losing thousands of dollars at a fake festival in a cow pasture in Montana, with your hands shoved into a big bag of poop? I laughed till I cried.

Now, years later when I reflect on that day, I think of Jimmy and his worm joy and how I've never laughed harder. He was my gift on a seemingly giftless day. The kind I would have never prayed for or thought up myself—but a gift all the same. A half-baked miracle of sorts.

OxiClean Miracles

In the town where I attended college, there was a church that led students on a mission trip to Mexico each year during spring break. Upon their return, stories would circulate around campus about the miracles the students experienced on the trip. A blind boy receiving eyesight, a paralyzed man walking for the first time, a baby at death's door suddenly recovering and thriving. I've been to Mexico, Africa, and all over Eastern Europe on different mission trips and have seen amazing men and women use their skills to tend to the needs of the most broken people. Building houses, collecting trash, holding orphans, drilling wells, and bandaging the wounds of the sick. I've seen firsthand the miracle of humans showing up for one another. But beyond that radical love, which is perhaps the most profound miracle of all, I've never seen the kinds of grandiose physical healings that the kids in college seemed to experience.

I am not qualified to talk about the type of miracle where a leg grows back, a baby lives against all odds, or a million dollars is discovered and financial limitations are suddenly solved. Not because I don't believe those things happen but because to the best of my knowledge, they have never happened to me. Many of the miracles in my life have occurred in the wake of tragedy and misfortune, when the miracle I so desperately prayed for did *not* happen. I get the feeling this is the case for many people. It's been in the dying and not-so-happily-ever-after moments that I have found myself elbows deep in worm poop, awed by the grace I am experiencing in the most unlikely places.

If you have eyes to see, the whole world is full of worm poop. Sometimes the miracle looks more like a Band-Aid put on with extraordinary love than a cure. Realizing that the miracle at hand often looks different from what I thought it would be has freed me to notice tiny moments of grace abounding everywhere.

I recently met a lady at one of my shows who wanted to tell me that her ordinary miracle was OxiClean. Her husband had lost his job, and they were struggling to keep food on the table and household staples in their home. "Whoever decided baseball uniforms should be white never did a load of laundry in their lives!" she told me through laughter and tears. OxiClean was the only product that would keep her son's baseball uniforms clean, and for the first time in her adult life, she couldn't afford to buy it. Well, someone gave her a coupon for OxiClean that they weren't going to use, and then she got another coupon out of the blue in the mail. She went to the store and found OxiClean on sale with an additional in-store coupon, and by the time it was all said and done, she had bought the store out of all the product they had and ended up *making* money off the purchase. "I'd rather my husband be able to find work, but until then, this is my miracle," she said.

Sometimes OxiClean is the gift. Little half-baked miracles.

Fix It

In the fifth chapter of the Gospel of John, Jesus asks a chronically sick man if he wants to be made well. To those who would listen for His voice today, Jesus asks the same question.

Do you want to be made well?

"Yes! Let the babies live!"

"Yes! Cure the cancer!"

"Yes! Restore the marriage!"

Yes. We plead, bargain, and barter with Jesus. "Fix our bodies. Change our situations." Our obsession lies with what we can see and quantify, what we can hold and touch and love. After all, these are the bodies, souls, babies, and covenant relationships that God Himself called good. There is nothing more human than the desire for a healed body or a restored relationship; it is the one common theme that has united people from every time period, ethnicity, age, and corner of the earth. We will go to great lengths to find a cure. But perhaps in our zealous quests to live long and prosper, we have confused Jesus' invitation to be made well with our own desire for fully cured bodies, and in doing so, we have altogether missed a deeper knowing of what it means to be healed by the Savior.

Our idea of healing has been one-dimensional for so long that we struggle to conceptualize any other form of healing outside the physical realm. We want big, grand, life-saving miracles! We don't pray for OxiClean and worm poop. Our requests are bold and asked with full confidence. And I imagine God loves our tenacity and faithfulness. The Bible itself invites us to come boldly before the throne and ask God to meet all our needs. But if we can only perceive God's mighty-showing-up power in the big and bold moments, we miss the potential healing that still comes when *big* and *bold* don't happen. When our greatest desire is for the temporal to become immortal, our idea of a miracle often becomes limited to the broken thing being fixed. We are tempted to equate God's presence in our lives with broken things being put perfectly back together.

The problem with this, of course, is that sometimes the broken things aren't fixed here and now. Sometimes the marriage ends, the babies die, the job is lost, the life savings are cleaned out, the disease grows, and the miracle you prayed for doesn't happen. When Jesus asks the paralyzed man at Bethesda if he wants to be made well, He is offering a timeless invitation for all believers. Do we want to be whole? The collective human answer is a resounding YES! *Fix our fractured fragments.* But how do we find healing when the broken situations aren't fixed the way we thought they would be? The Great Physician comes with the offer to make us well despite the knowledge that there is no cure for our mortality and some earthly things will remain broken. This lets me know there is more to being made well than the curing of our bodies or fixing of our situations. There is wholeness to be found on the roads we never prayed for.

Completely Other Ways

I will not stop believing in medical cures and unexplainable, physical miracles. I will never stop asking God for relationships to be redeemed and restored this side of heaven. I will always hope and believe in faith for these things. But I will not rest my ability to be made whole in their hands. Miracles happen, cures are discovered, and seemingly impossible situations and relationships are redeemed and restored here and now. *But even if they are not,* my ability for wholeness is not diminished or stolen. Far beyond the curing of our bodies or the fixing of our temporal situations, God is in the business of making us well in completely other ways.

Jesus liked to make people well. He didn't tell them there was no hope for them until the afterlife. And He didn't begin their healing by evaluating their diets, fitness routines, sex lives, stock portfolios, or mental fortitude. He went right past the surface, deep inside the heart, and set them on the course toward salvation—the path of wholeness. Perhaps that path ultimately has much less to do with the condition of the body than we would like to believe. For those touched by Jesus throughout Scripture, He sought more than their physical health; He sought healing that led to wholeness. The same is true for you and me. He seeks more than just our health; He seeks our healing.

While it may seem like a half-baked miracle—the one that comes without the physical cure we so often hope and pray for—the miracle of healing is that we can be made well and whole regardless of what happens to our bodies or the outcome of our life situations. If cancer comes and cancer conquers, my ability to be made whole is not diminished. If my marriage dissolves, my daughter dies, or my career crumbles—there is healing to be found. If my lingering mental illness is never miraculously cured, I can *still* be made well.

I have to repeat this to myself often. I can be made well even if _____ happens this side of heaven. Just like Shadrach, Meshach, and Abednego professed before King Nebuchadnezzar, who threatened to throw the men into a blazing fire pit if they did not abandon their Jewish faith and bow down to his gods of gold, "The God whom we serve is able to save us. . . . *But even if he doesn't* . . . we will never serve your gods or worship the gold statue you have set up."[1] Those guys were on to something. They knew God was able to miraculously save, but more important, they understood that even if they didn't see a great big flashy miracle, they could still entrust themselves to God's care.

Healing happens when we entrust ourselves to God's care and become aware of the miraculous ways He is at work in our midst, binding the wounds. While we yell "Fix it!" and shake our fists at the lack of response, God is often quietly at work behind the scenes answering in ways we would never expect or pray for. The ways that come small, steady, and whispery in the dark of night, in the depths of pain. The ways that aren't always flashy and grand.

I know very little about the body being radically cured or great big giant miracles, but I've learned a thing or two about healing. The kind that happens when the miracle you prayed for doesn't. Healing often occurs in spite of grandiose miracles and cures. It happens as we embark on the journey that leads us back to our original wholeness, and we encounter Emmanuel walking alongside us, reminding us that we are His beloved.

Beloved

One year at Thanksgiving dinner my three-year-old niece, Lexie, and her stuffed animal named Lamby reminded me that Jesus liked me from the beginning. Lamby is a tiny blanket with a stuffed lamb sewn to the top, and she goes everywhere with my niece. As I watched Lexie interact with Lamby, I realized how loving and caring this inanimate object was to everyone she encountered. Lamby always shares, gives kisses, and tells people how much she loves them. To my own daughter she exclaimed, "You're my favorite, and I am going to give you a kiss right now!" and then the worn-out, dingy animal kissed her on the head.

Impressed by the loving nature of Lamby, I wanted my niece to know what an amazing mom Lamby must have to act with such kindness. Hoping to affirm and build her up, I began to praise Lamby's mom, when my niece quickly interrupted me and quietly said, "Jesus made Lamby perfect before I even knew her. Before I even knew Jesus. He made her perfect and that's why she's so good. Jesus made her good."

The room grew silent. We were stunned. Not only does my niece speak as though she has known Jesus for a while, she reminds us that Lamby is good because Jesus made her that way. And that's all there is to it. I am grateful for that beat-up stuffed animal and the tiny little girl holding it, reminding me that Jesus made us good.

What is most true about me is the image of God inside of me. *Imago Dei* is my starting point and my finish line. My birthmark, my DNA. Before anything else was set in motion, there was a Jenny, and she was made well. Before anything else in your life was set in motion, there was a *you*, and you were made well. Our origin, heritage, and inheritance were given to us freely by the very hands that fearfully and wonderfully created us. God called us *good*.

A Tarnished Narrative

We have been told otherwise by well-meaning voices longing to lead us to Jesus. Jesus, they say, will pave the way for God to like us and allow God to tolerate the same air space as us.

I once shared the stage with a pastor who began his sermon by telling the audience that God hated them. People nodded their heads readily in affirmation of what they apparently already knew to be true: they were despised. It was not personal, this pastor said; it was God's very nature to hate what was not holy. And since we were sinners in need of a Savior, God *had* to hate us until we were restored to Him through Jesus.

I cringed on the side of the stage. I was at once angry and sad. Tears began to slide down my unclean cheeks. Hated by the Holy? What do I know of Holy? Not a whole lot, to tell you the truth. But enough to know I am not hated by my own Creator. I was, in fact, formed by God's good hands and spoken into existence by His creativity—I am the *offspring* of the Creator. How can a holy God who is light create darkness? He cannot. I am lovely because God loves me. A good God who longs to restore His children to Himself does not create broken and flawed children. This is a story of rescue and redemption, not a story of holy hate.

Darkness is inside of me, to be sure. Monumental mistakes, regret, shame, fear, worry, and that testy temper of mine are all there, fighting to take over my insides, rushing for the reins to rule my mind and body. My brokenness is well documented in the caverns of my soul; my sin nature is fastened well into place. But before and underneath that, the very core of my essence is not darkness, it is light. Adam and Eve ate the apple and opened our eyes to a condition less than Edenic, plunging us into sin. But their sin wasn't original. *They* were original. Before our brokenness rears its head, we are first and foremost created, shaped, formed, and hemmed together in our mother's womb by an Artist who does not create broken art. The Artist creates art that reflects Him—we are the signature brushstrokes and design of God's hands. We were created for wholeness.

I recently led a high school girls' retreat at a church. A seventeen-year-old approached me at the end of the weekend and said, "I became a Christian later than most of the girls here—I was fifteen years old. I always loved myself before I became a Christian, but now I feel like I constantly hear about all the ways I am broken, how sinful I am, and why I should be worried for myself and the world. I just wanted to thank you for not coming in here and listing all the reasons we are separated from God but telling us that God is close and finds joy in us. It made me think maybe this whole God thing is about more than just what's wrong with me and everyone else."

My heart broke for her and for the entire Christian family. Somehow we have turned God's best creation—His children— into something so broken and inherently sinful that we no longer know how to exclaim that we are *proudly made* by God Himself. We have cultivated a culture of believers who far too readily label themselves as damaged and totally depraved and cannot identify their connection to the umbilical cord that fed and sustained their earliest, innate identity in Christ. Knowing God means we know with more certainty than anyone our origin.

My True Identity

When I think about reconnecting to my original design, I remember Robin Williams in the movie *Hook*. Williams plays an overworked, stressed-out, uncaring father who does not remember that before he became the man he currently is, he was Peter Pan. The movie becomes a journey of rediscovery as Williams's character, Peter Banning, flies to Neverland to rescue his children from Captain Hook. In one particularly poignant scene, Peter still has no idea of his boyhood identity; he has been harassed, is exhausted, and is very near giving up when a little boy walks up to him and begins to touch his face. The boy takes Peter's cheeks into his hands and stretches them one way and then another. The Lost Boys watch in hushed silence. He touches Peter's eyebrows and stretches tight the skin on his cheekbones until he catches a glimpse of the *real* Peter Pan and recognizes who he truly is. A knowing smile breaks out on the little boy's face as he says, "Oh, there you are, Peter." The other Lost Boys gather around, looking intently, touching his face, recognizing him for who he really is, and saying, "There you are, Peter. There you are!" I cry every time Peter Banning remembers his true identity as Peter Pan.

Remembering who you are changes everything. When you have forgotten who you are and where your home is, there is nothing sweeter than the hands of heaven reaching out to remind you of your true identity. Author James Bryan Smith says, "May we have the courage not to run when the voice of our condemning heart would tear us from the place where we can hear the voice of God saying to us, 'You are my beloved child, in whom I am well pleased.' Even if our hearts condemn us, God is greater than our hearts."[1]

The longer I know Jesus, the more I realize He is reminding me of *who I am* versus who I am not. He points to all that is already within me. I go to Jesus because in Him I sense I am more than I know and get the feeling He is waiting for me to look in the mirror and see myself for who I truly am: an image bearer of God. I wonder what happens when we stop banging the gong and confessing how miserably broken we are and instead find Jesus waiting for us to rediscover who we have been all along: His beloved.

Beloved

As the pastor spoke all those years ago, I am sure it sounded quite theologically astute to begin by telling those gathered that God hated them. It certainly got our attention, the way a cheap gimmick does. But my soul ached for Jesus Himself to swing the doors wide open, walk among those two thousand college students, the major leaders of the church, and the theologian with fury in his voice, and speak the words that He spoke to the ragtag men, women, and children who followed Him when He walked the earth two thousand years ago: "you are light," "My sheep," "sons and daughters," "no longer servants—I call you friend."[2] Those are the words Jesus used to describe His offspring. Not hated, but *created* by God. Chosen. Set apart. Delighted in.

What is most original to you and me? I have to ask myself that a lot. In a church culture that sometimes seems more willing to tell me how depraved and broken I am, I pause to ask Jesus, "Who do You say I am?" He knows my sin and broken bits. No one knows my humanity better than the One who took it upon Himself to free me from it. He took my prone-to-wander nature so that I might be reconnected to the God who made me and called me good in the first place. He and God conspired to bring about a love story where lost children remember their original identity and find rescue. Because of this, I am free to peel back my earth layers and live from my God nature. At my core, what is most true about me is not my darkness but my light.

Maybe you have heard that you were hated by God, or like the seventeen-year-old girl, you've found the church to be the very source from which the obsession over your brokenness springs forth. Enough already. The Creator did not dip His paintbrush in the black vial of Satan's paint and draw the strokes of our core from the palette of another artist. You were not created broken before you ever had a chance to become beautiful.

We were created whole through God's holiness—made well in God's very image and nature. Like Lamby, we were called good because Jesus made us that way. Formed, brought to life, desired, designed, and delighted in by an artist who needed colors from no one but Himself. He created the colors, splattered them on the palette, and began painting life into existence. To believe this, Rachel Held Evans says, is one of our biggest hurdles: "The great struggle of the Christian life is to take God's name for us, to believe we are beloved and to believe that is enough."[3]

My mom recently texted me on my birthday to say, "I remember the day you were born. I loved you even before I knew you." She is not the only one who feels this way about me. My God feels this way too. I have known it since I was a little girl. Perhaps I learned it before I knew how to spell my name. My memory is shaky, but I recall the whispers of divine love more clearly than anything else in my life. Before I had a chance to impress, injure, insult, invest in, or invent the person whom others would come to know as Jenny, my God created me, knew me, and lavished His love upon me. "Our being known by God does not begin when we first recognize it or when we acknowledge it or even when we make our first struggling attempts to come to grips with what it might mean for the creator of the universe to know us and choose us," author Robert Benson says. "It begins at the beginning, when we are first imagined into being."[4]

You were imagined into being by the Creator of the universe. You were given life from God's very essence. The road toward wholeness is a returning to a place we once knew—not a departure to a foreign land. Sally Lloyd Jones says this about Adam and Eve's separation from God: "Though they would forget him, and run from him, deep in their hearts, God's children would miss him always, and long for him—lost children yearning for their home."[5] Perhaps we are all lost children yearning for our real home. Yearning to be made well as we live in the tension of the now—but the not yet. The journey of being made well is our homecoming.

Holey, Holey, Holey

This is what I know about life so far:

Always pee sooner rather than later.

Anticipate seasonal product change or you will completely miss out on Target's Dollar Spot deals.

Tell your people you love them.

And count on death. It's seriously always creeping up, rearing its ugly head.

Life is *so* deathy. We were created whole and made well by God in the first place. But it doesn't take long for the brokenness to creep in. Sometimes it feels like the laundry list of pain is never ending, and perhaps more often than ever before it seems death dominates our daily newsfeeds.

I was twelve years old when I walked into the hospital room where my aunt lay dying. It was my first taste of death. With a homemade construction-paper card shaking in my hands, I was trapped between two worlds. Both a little girl and an almost teenager, I was trying to navigate knowing and not wanting to know the painful realities of the world.

Aunt Debbie was my creative hero and the only other left-handed person in our family. I was convinced this meant we shared a secret bond. She told me we were the creative force of the universe. I believed her and felt special. She gave me the courage to be uniquely me. Her laughter infused others with an electric, contagious energy. She smiled wide as we walked into her hospital room and never let on that she was letting go. But I was painfully aware this was good-bye.

I remember every detail of her funeral. The moment our family was ushered into the funeral home in New Orleans to see her body. The buckling of knees and the wail that came out of my Mamaw; the grief that caused my Papaw to sob as he held his daughter's cold face in his hands and kissed her over and over again in that horrible room. Aaron Neville's voice rang through the air on a CD as he sang words that would bury themselves in my soul and haunt me: "I bid you goodnight." The grief I tasted in that room never left me.

Unborn babies and stillborn babies. Accidents, suicide, young moms who die from cancer, the childhood disease no one saw coming. Violent deaths mar our newsfeed so frequently we have become immune. Domestic murder, mass shootings, suicide bombings, planes dropping from the sky. Bullets. Every day there are more bullets, and war rages on in seemingly every corner of the earth. In a somber sermon given at the beginning of Advent, Pope Francis said, "Christmas is approaching: there will be lights, parties, Christmas trees and nativity scenes—but it's all a charade. The world continues to go to war. The world has not chosen a peaceful path. . . . We should ask for the grace to weep for this world, which does not recognize the path to peace. To weep for those who live for war and have the cynicism to deny it." He added, "God weeps, Jesus weeps."[1] The ache of death is everywhere. Our collective soul is sick. We would do well to ask for the grace to weep.

As if the physical body dying were not enough to contend with, there are other deaths in this life we must walk through as well. The death of marriages, friendships, dreams, careers, relationships, stages of life, sanity, and health. Nineteenth-century theologian Ian Maclaren implores us, "Be kind, for everyone you meet is fighting a hard battle."[2] He's right. So many are grieving, wounded, tired, and sad—we are all fighting battles. At some point in our lives, we all need healing. Bidding goodnight to the people, relationships, and things we hold most dear takes a toll on our souls and leaves holes, every single time.

We Are Many

When I was touring the country with my band, Addison Road, we spent most weeks crammed into a sixteen-passenger van, driving from city to city, eating terrible fast food. When we weren't in a van together, we lived in a tiny condo in Dallas. *All five of us.* It was the kind of thing you did because you were naively, zealously in your twenties and you could.

One summer we left for a string of shows and returned weeks later to find that the most horrific smell had infiltrated our condo. We gagged out loud and frantically ran around the tiny space flinging open windows, randomly spraying Febreze into the air, and searching for dead bodies. But it was to no avail; we could not find the culprit and the smell lingered.

Hours later our landlord came over to check the attic and crawl space because we'd assured him something, somewhere, had died. Upon arrival, he agreed. He scoured the attic and went underneath the home but couldn't find the source of the smell either.

Eventually our noses adjusted, but the odor lingered. If you had to leave the condo for any reason, the torture of reacclimating to the scent of death started all over again upon arrival.

Several days into the ordeal I went to cook a TV dinner in the microwave and found the source of all our problems: broccoli cheese casserole. Before we left on our trip, one of the guys had put broccoli cheese casserole in the microwave and forgotten about it. For three weeks that casserole grew in the humid heat of a Texas summer. It actually *grew*. Mold and fungus covered the walls of the microwave in wave after wave of frothy blue and black foam. I nearly vomited. We brought the microwave outside, knowing it could not be salvaged and should probably only be handled by someone wearing a hazmat suit. Mold had run wild, and the smell permeated everything.

If left alone to fester in the dormancy of our souls, unhealed wounds start burrowing down inside of us, creating holes. Like cancer cells, or forgotten broccoli cheese casserole in a hot Texas microwave, our holes can multiply and spread if left alone. Holes beget holes. Over time unhealed places can turn us into the worst possible versions of ourselves. What grows out of those *holey*, unhealed places varies from person to person but can often take on behaviors that look like abuse, addiction, affairs, an anxious spirit, anger, control, comparison, divorce, envy, gluttony, hopelessness, manipulation, materialism, pride, ungratefulness, or soul paralysis, to name a few.

In the Gospel of Mark, Jesus encounters a man possessed by a demonic spirit roaming through the town's cemetery. When Jesus approaches the man and asks his name, the demon replies, "My name is Legion, for we are many."[3]

Over the years, my holes have become many. Though I am *the beloved*, I am not always well and I am far from whole. My God-given identity spoken over me at conception is not what I am prone to live by. I am prone to wander. And this world takes its hits. Just like the man running wild through the cemetery whose demons hissed, "We are many," sometimes the holes in our own lives run wild yelling the same thing. *We are many.*

Our holes stem from every source imaginable and come in all shapes and sizes. The physical holes of mental illness handed down to me, like a gift-wrapped animal eating its way out of a package under the Christmas tree. ADHD, generalized anxiety disorder, and a peculiar form of obsessive-compulsive disorder have been with me since I was a little girl. They taunt me. *We are many*, they say. The emotional holes from the painful deaths of loved ones, my unfaithful spirit, my own sin, broken friendships, and corrupt motives. The spiritual holes from the shallowness I've fed off of in the celebrity Christian culture. The pain inflicted on me by churches in my past. My own doubts and disillusionments as I often wrestle with threadbare faith. I long to be holy, yet I find myself riddled with holes. I'm *holey*.

Bad Days

My healing journey began in my early twenties, right around the time I found the broccoli cheese casserole in the microwave. As I discovered my own demons, dealt with a volatile marriage, and tried to process through years of anger that I had held on to—the hard work of healing seemed *too* hard. Afraid, lonely, and angry that I even had to work for health when no one else around me seemed to be tasked with that, I started secretly praying for escape routes. My prayers became devoted to the hope that I would be in a semi-major yet non-life-threatening car wreck, and I might have prayed about heart attacks. *For other people.*

It's horrible to confess, I know. This is why I go to therapy and spend a lot of time in church. I don't want to be the kind of girl who prays for car wrecks and heart attacks. I want to pray for light and life and blessings. But sometimes that's hard because I've got the *holey* syndrome. And when my attempts at being healthy don't seem to pan out or the path becomes too laborious, the temptation to swing clear across to the other side creeps into my soul. Maybe digging my feet deeper into sickness, loss, victimization, and unhealthiness will bring me the things I ultimately need to find healing? Maybe by becoming sicker, I can get the attention I need to become well again? Sometimes we stay sick because we have no idea how to make our way to the hands of healing or just don't want to do the hard work to get there. Living with holes seems easier.

You might know what it's like to live with holes too. Perhaps you battle mental illness, physical decay, a life-altering diagnosis, or you live with the constant pain of ruptured and unrepaired relationships. Maybe death feels easier than life. A teeny-tiny car wreck that would safely deliver you to a hospital and the watchful care of nurses sounds more bearable than that other painful thing that never seems to go away. It may not be cancer of the cells you're dealing with, but cancer of the soul. Seasons when hate is palpable, exhaustion evident, depression damning, and patience painfully nonexistent. Seasons when you have nothing left to give the world but prayers that they will *all have heart attacks*. It's a wild hunch, but you might be in need of healing if you find yourself wishing for a quiet crumbling of your current existence or the existence of others. Heart attacks and car wrecks? These are cheap solutions for deep pain, the groanings of unwell people who desperately need to be made whole.

During those dark moments in my twenties when I was hoping for a car wreck or short-term disease, I was *not* finding healing in a healthy way. Today those same thoughts creep into my mind from time to time the way a glass of bourbon creeps into a twenty-years-sober alcoholic's mind. Who doesn't want a shortcut to ease the pain, a quick fix to feed the craving? When the hard work of healing feels *too* hard and you just want it to be easy already, sometimes double pneumonia and a few nights in the hospital seem like a decent answer. More food, sex, parties, pills, promotions, working out, TV binging, gifts, angry emails, charges on the credit card, or vacations—maybe those will heal?

Not seeing a way forward or knowing how to deal with feelings that fester just below the surface of an unwell heart, a sick person will go to great lengths to numb the pain. But when a person pleads for escape routes, what they are often pleading for is a catalyst toward healing. A way forward. We want to be well; we just don't always know how to get there.

Better Days

On my better days, I attempt to solve the holey-ness issue by making ambitious resolutions toward being a healthy person. The problem is, *healthy* can mean any number of things. My wanting to be healthy could mean I want to lose ten pounds, have a stronger heart, eat better foods, or attempt to be vegan, gluten free, dairy free, sugar free, fat free, or somehow, magically, food free. These attempts at becoming healthy all sound like personal versions of hell. (I think it should be noted that *hell* rhymes with *kale* for a reason. Mind you, it only rhymes if you are from the South, but that's beside the point. Was kale even a real-life food ten years ago?)

Healthy could mean the desire to be spiritually attuned, emotionally balanced, or at peace with dolphins and endangered rhinos. It can mean I vaccinate or don't vaccinate my children, have babies in a bathtub at home or in a hospital surrounded by doctors and modern medicine. Being healthy could mean having proper emotional boundaries, a great sex life, or a robust stock portfolio. Say the word *healthy* in a CrossFit gym, chemo ward, graduate school psychology class, or to a parent watching their child cross the finish line at the Special Olympics, and gauge their answers. What is *healthy* anyway?

Ultimately, I often chase physical health because I believe it will lead to healing. Those holes that are many? I don't want them. So I pour myself into healthy lifestyle regimens: a different diet, workout, essential oil, supplement, or fitness accomplishment. I strive for health but get no closer to being healed than I did with the last fad. Though often well intentioned, my attempts at healing are shortsighted when they solely revolve around the size of my hips, firmness of my arms, or quality of food I grab from the grocery store. Being healthy is certainly part of being made well, but it is not the whole.

A person can actually be healthy without ever being healed. *Healthy* and *healing* are not synonymous. The common definition for *healthy* is "enjoying or possessing good health and vigor of body, mind, or spirit." Whereas *healing* literally means "to make whole."[4] One is a possession, the other a process. One a destination, the other a journey. Healing is the pilgrimage through which we are made well. When my attempts for healing get confused and tangled up with simply being a healthy person, the results fall short of holy healing.

Reverend Becca Stevens, founder of Thistle Farms and the Magdalene Community for sexually exploited women, writes about her own healing path from sexual abuse in her book *Snake Oil*. "The journey of healing is not a fairy tale but a long story of transformation that inspires us all to keep seeking healing," she says.[5] More often than not, healing is a prolonged process, not an instant, magical fix. It's a book with many chapters.

The road toward wholeness is long and winding.

I am encouraged by the words of Romans 12, which implore us not to be conformed to the patterns of this world but be transformed by the renewing of our minds. Our path is not throw-the-towel-in conformity but renewed transformation. And transformation takes time. Healing is a hard and holy excursion, not a fairy tale. But the central invitation of the gospel is to be restored to our original wholeness—to the image of Christ. And that is God's work. He transforms the holes. We are simply invited to accept the invitation and allow God Himself to tend to our wounds, that we might know regenerated life on the other side of our holey-ness.

Invitations

Over the years, as my music has found its way into people's stories, I have been on the receiving end of a profound range of bizarre and beautiful invitations into their lives and ministries. I will always remember the invitation to travel to South Sudan with World Concern, a humanitarian aid organization that I deeply admire and respect. Sleeping in a mosquito net, going to the bathroom on the side of a dirt road in a field full of baboons, and driving to the most remote villages on earth to watch this organization tend to the needs of the world's most vulnerable tribes was one of the greatest joys of my life.

As we prepared to leave one South Sudanese village, a severely malnourished woman held her tiny baby up to me and said, "Take, take." I shook my head no. I could not take her child, but I leaned over to kiss the baby on her forehead. With one hand, the momma pulled her tunic open to reveal her deflated breasts. "No milk, no milk. Take. Take," she insistently repeated. She continued to beg as we got in the back of our rugged vehicle and drove away, never once breaking eye contact with me. The invitation to take the child so that she might live wrecked my soul.

I will never forget the socially awkward teenage girl who told me her life story after a concert and finished by saying, "Want to see my scar?" Before I could answer, "Thank you for the invitation, but no thanks," she lifted her shirt and a few layers of belly fat to point out where her appendix had been taken out. "You wanna touch it?" she exclaimed with her thick Texas accent. Nope. No thank you. I have to maintain *some* standards.

Or on a different day, to the shock of those around us, the woman who nearly took her shirt off in an autograph line to show me the tattoo of her daughter's face, which wrapped from her back, around her breast, and down to her stomach and was encircled by the words to one of our band's songs. She'd commissioned the artwork after her daughter's murder. Although it was probably an inappropriate moment to take her shirt off, it was a sincerely moving invitation into her grieving process.

Once, our band was invited to tour NASA's headquarters in Houston, Texas, alongside an astronaut who had recently been to outer space and brought our CD along for the ride. I think this means we were *technically* invited to outer space. We were joined on the tour by another man who works on the floor of mission control. He invited us beyond the glass, where friends and family sit, onto the actual floor. For a girl who has watched the movie *Apollo 13* at least a thousand times, this was a dream come true.

One of the most profound moments of my life happened as I stood on the floor of mission control and listened in and watched while two astronauts on the space station joked around and detailed their experiments with recumbent bikes to the ground crew within arm's length of me. It looked just like the movies. There were floor-to-ceiling screens showing the earth, time zones, the slow roll of orbit, and the movement of the space station. All of a sudden, as I stared at planet earth—which was so teeny-tiny compared to the vastness of space surrounding it—peace seemed plausible. I felt the Holy Spirit whisper, *It's not so big after all. You all are closer than you think.* And from that moment on my vision changed and the world seemed smaller in the best ways. Maybe we weren't as divided and fragmented as I had come to believe. Perhaps there was more keeping us together on this little planet than tearing us apart.

Oh, the invitations we receive over the course of our lives! Whether spoken or unspoken, they are the gateway to every single experience we have. We can be afraid of them and turn them down or endeavor to say yes—though they may seem bizarre, far-flung, or out of our comfort zone.

Life is one grand invitation. Starting in the womb, we are invited to take up residency inside another human. We are invited to feed from the umbilical cord that unites us to our mother's body, taking the very nutrients she offers. After birth we are invited to live. Given carte blanche! We can grow, learn, thrive, bloom, and flourish. But we can also quit. Failure to thrive is real, both in babies *and* in adults. Besides our arrival on planet earth, which we had no say in, every moment thereafter is a grand invitation to live if we so choose. But we must choose; living fully is never forced upon us. Neither is the pilgrimage toward healing.

God says He stands at the door of our hearts and knocks, and that if we hear His voice and open the door for Him, He will come in and we will eat tacos together.[1] He doesn't actually mention tacos, but I assume this is what He means by wanting to share a meal with me in particular. It's a standing offer to open the door of my life and create space at the table for the King. He doesn't barge in, but knocks and waits while we contemplate the invitation at hand.

Quitting Is an Option

One summer during college, I volunteered to take care of babies in a Romanian orphanage. Before traveling overseas, we went through extensive training on the conditions we would likely encounter in these children who had been neglected since birth. Without proper touch, babies will begin to rock themselves back and forth and lick the walls just to get the stimulation their bodies need. Nothing can prepare you for seeing a six-month-old use all their might to push up on their forearms and begin licking the rusty, metal crib they are lying in. But they did it time and again.

My heart broke for these babies, but even more so for one little boy named Sebastian who quickly became my favorite. Sebastian was two years old with brown eyes the shape of olives. By all standards he should have been able to walk and talk, but he wasn't. Among a room of ten babies, he was the least active. There were two mattresses on the floor where the ten kids were placed each morning. Caretakers roamed the halls as the babies lay on the dirty mattresses babbling to one another. They took the best care of the children that they could, but ten mommas in a building with more than one hundred babies wears thin.

While Vlad, Ionela, Dan, and the crew of other tinies in my room rooted around for bottles, rocked themselves, and babbled on the mattresses, Sebastian lay quietly curled in the fetal position, sucking two fingers, with a far-off gaze in his eyes. He was alive, but not really. He had my heart completely, and his responsiveness became my mission.

When I met Sebastian, the weight of neglect hovered over his body and soul, and for reasons beyond his control or choosing, his spirit was giving up. He was a textbook case of failure to thrive. But when engaged and invited to live, he gradually began to fight back. Slowly, life emerged inside of him. By the end of the summer he was scooting, muttering, and most importantly, smiling. I prayed for his future and poured every ounce of love I possessed into him. I told him I was proud of him. I must have whispered it a million times in his ears.

I often find myself encouraging people during the hardest moments on their road toward healing by telling them I am proud of them. The response is almost universal: "But I'm not doing anything to be proud of. I'm just surviving."

"Yeah, but surviving is a choice," I tell them. "You are here! You are breathing when you could very well be on the floor in a diaper, convulsing, refusing to move, unwilling or unable to walk through the moment at hand. And that's enough to be proud of." They usually laugh and think I'm being dramatic. But what they don't yet understand is that they have accepted the invitation to keep living when they don't have to. No one is forcing them. They could just as well curl up in the fetal position and simply quit. Though it is not what we were created for, nor is it the path of life-giving transformation, quitting is a legitimate option to the invitation of life. Realizing that you *haven't* given up when it is indeed an option can fuel your confidence as you press into the hard seasons. You are walking! Or crawling! Or at the very least breathing, and that *is* something.

After my nieces died, people at shows would often ask about my sister to see how she was doing. Truth is, she and her husband knew they would have to wage the biggest war of their lives to keep living after their daughters' deaths, and they attacked the healing process immediately on multiple fronts. But my general response was, "Well, she got out of bed today—and in my book, that is a win." As humanity's best cheerleader, author Glennon Melton, says, knowing that you can do hard things makes all the difference in the world. Life isn't easy. If you are living and breathing and getting out of bed each day, or every other day for that matter, you deserve a cupcake.

A neglected baby who has never known the love of a mother or father cannot be expected to get up off their mattress and accept the invitation to choose life. They have none of the tools needed to survive and thrive. The sickest and most vulnerable among us are often in the same position; they can no more accept the invitation to journey toward healing than they can make their holes disappear. But most of us are not in that position. We have the means to accept the invitation to live. We can open the door of our hearts to God's healing love. The choice to pick up our mats and move forward, even in the midst of great pain or seemingly insurmountable odds, is within our grasp. Saying yes to that choice, no matter how small the yes may be, is a huge accomplishment. Everyone needs a cheerleader encouraging them with this truth. So if no one else is speaking these words over you right now, let me: *I am proud of you. You can do hard things. You are still breathing, and that is enough. And you are so loved.*

Accepting Your Invitation

When it comes to our healing journeys, nothing—even death itself—forces us to accept the invitation to be made well.

Experiencing healing and being made well are not the natural by-products of pain. They are by-products of a decision—a choice—to be made well. We are invited into this process, never forced. And it is the acceptance of the invitation to embark on a holy voyage toward healing that leads to our eventual wholeness.

In the Gospel of John, Jesus visits a place where sick people gather around pools of water waiting for their chance to be healed. The waters at Bethesda were well known for their healing powers. Occasionally they were stirred, and the people believed angels or spirits of some sort would heal the first person to touch the water. With the hindsight of human discovery and science on our side, we now know the stirring was likely the bubbling effect a geyser or spring makes when coming forth from the surface. But back then it might as well have been the healing hand of Asclepius. They were not missing this opportunity. Sick people settled in, guarded their spot, and fought for their chance to be made well.

On the particular day we see Jesus visiting Bethesda, He encounters a man who has been unwell for thirty-eight years. Thirty-eight years of pain. Can you imagine? Maybe you can. There has to be a special place in heaven for people who have endured thirty-eight years without relief of their physical and mental pain. Jesus looks the man in the eyes and says exactly what *I do not want Jesus to say*. "Do you want to be made well?" He asks.[2] And every time I read this I am annoyed. Does he *want* to? Are you kidding me? He's been unwell for thirty-eight years. What kind of question is that, Jesus? Don't ask—just heal!

Were it up to me and my finite, shallow wisdom, I would want Jesus to walk straight up to the unwell person and say with an overly dramatic Southern accent, "Oh my gosh, you poor thing. Let me fix that for you! No, no, no, sweetie. Don't say a word, I'll just take care of this right now. You sit still and let me work my Jesus power." Then Jesus would do some sort of abracadabra chant and voilà, make it all better. This is the God that my human head tries to create.

But what Jesus does here is vitally important. He bypasses my desire for cheap grace and quick fixes and does what He does best—He invites. Jesus doesn't assume the man wants to be made well—He knows some people prefer to stay sick. He doesn't cast blame for the man's illness, pontificate on sin and sanctification, offer an easy formula or quick fix. Instead, Jesus looks into the eyes of a deeply wounded man and offers an invitation. "Do you want to be made well?"

Sometimes we must force ourselves to choose the invitation of healing when the people around us would just as soon *never* see us healed. Whether consciously or subconsciously, these people have created an unhealthy system that depends on everyone around them staying sick and bound up. Finding freedom that enables you to move forward threatens their system. Your oppression is vital to the codependent operation they have created. Your healing threatens to undo their stronghold. If you are made well, those around you are confronted with their own ability to be made well. Author Amber Haines reminds us, "The healing and wholeness of one brings healing and wholeness of the community."[3] And many times this is beautifully true; redemption of the whole is the hope of the gospel. But sadly, it is not always the case.

In his book *Prototype*, Pastor Jonathan Martin talks about the people who watched Jesus heal the demon-possessed man of Gerasene and their seeming fear of being made well themselves:

> In a world where self-destructive behavior has become commonplace, the most frightening scenario may not be a global apocalypse. Perhaps the most startling thing to see is someone

whom we have come to expect to be as fragmented, fractured, and self-destructive as we are, transformed into the epitome of sanity, peace, and purpose.

We're afraid, not because we would rather see the demonized man continue to harm himself—we're terrified because his transformation raises for us new possibilities for what it means to be human.[4]

My being made well might shine a light on someone close to me who is also sick. It might raise the possibility of *their* potential to be made well. This could be the start of a redemptive journey for them—the healing and wholeness of one bringing healing and wholeness to the entire community. But there is also a chance that the light might cause them to shrink back into the dark corners, where their eyes are plenty adjusted and they are comfortable in the cobwebs. They want me to stay sick because they are still sick. In this case, I must drown out the voices that wish to keep me entangled and listen for the whispered invitation of my Savior to be set free.

Healing, Jesus says, is our choice. Healing, He says, is a partnership. Equal parts divine grace and human willingness.

When the paralytic man finally understands what is being offered to him, not only is his body restored, but his soul is too. The same God who drew near to the man waiting by the waters of Bethesda comes to you and me with the invitation: "Do you want to be made well?"

The decision is ours.

Love Heals

Long before we are invited to be healed by God, we are invited to be loved by God. The healing journey begins *after* we surrender to God's love. When we finally come to accept the fact that we are madly, deeply, fully known and enjoyed by our Creator God, we are set free to begin our journey toward wholeness.

Before I embraced God's love for me, I was caught in a constant battle to prove myself, defend myself, embellish myself, and care for myself. Two decades of my Christian life were spent operating out of fear, merit, and selfishness. I believed the right things, but I didn't yet grasp how deep, how wide, how ridiculously forgiving and never ending the love of Christ was. I had known God's voice since I was a little girl—his whispers of love over me. But that was then, when my innocence morphed into self-righteousness and the worst parts of me showed up in my zealous attempts at being God's favorite. I was a Christian talking head who had no need for grace—until I did. And then I needed it desperately and wondered if God could still love a person like me.

In those dark moments, when my severe need for mercy was ever before me, His voice pierced my shame. It came through these exact words in the book *Embracing the Love of God*:

> I have called you by my name, from the very beginning. You are mine and I am yours. You are my Beloved, on you my favor rests. I have molded you from the depths of the earth and knitted you together in your mother's womb. I have carved you in the palms of my hands and hidden you in the shadow of my embrace. Has it crossed your mind that I am proud you have accepted the gift of faith I have offered you? Proud that you have freely chosen me, after I had chosen you, as your friend and Lord? Proud that with all your warts and wrinkles you haven't given up? I never expected that you would be perfect.
>
> I love you. I love you. I love you. Nothing will ever change that.[5]

As I sat in the midst of those things I never thought I would do, in those places I was sure Christ could not find me—He found me and dispelled my shame with His tender mercy. His love was fiercer than I remembered. His love heals. It is a radically vulnerable act to entertain the knowledge that you are fully known and fiercely loved by a God who finds favor in you. A God who likes you. But it is the starting point. And what a merciful place to start. Acceptance and love. God's invitation to me was clear: I was loved and I could live loved. Accepting that invitation was the gateway to being made well.

6

Psychiatrist, Therapist, Pills—Oh My!

I saw my first therapist when I was a senior in high school. He was severely obese, sweaty, and always standing up. Think Chris Farley's "Down by the River." I was there with my family because we were church casualties. I suppose all firings and forced resignations are difficult for families. But it feels intensely personal when it's a church. Those were the people with whom we shared meals, summer camp, space in our living room for weekly Bible studies, and places at our table when they faced their first holiday alone.

I grew up within the walls of the church, roaming hallways, belonging to everyone. After school, there were times when my sisters and I sat in people's living rooms while Mom went into the back bedroom to pray over someone in the congregation as they lay dying. Other days we would stay in the car doing homework while Mom sat on the front porch with someone who'd just found out they had cancer or whose spouse had left a note saying they weren't coming back. I pretended not to hear when a parent showed up at our front door around midnight, worried sick because their teenager hadn't come home, confessing through tears about the fights and pregnancy scares. This happened more times than I can count during my mom's twenty years of being a youth pastor. There wasn't a holiday that a starting-over, lonely person wasn't invited to sit at our family dinner table before heading to church with us for services. Being the child of a minister means you hear things and know things that the rest of the church doesn't. It's a beautiful curse. We belonged to everyone.

Then, suddenly, everyone grew quiet. And it felt as though we belonged to no one.

The denomination my parents were employed by offered free therapy for families caught in the middle of church conflict. I suppose there was some degree of comfort in knowing that we were not the first to walk these painful roads. Thinking back, I am not sure what we talked about in that brief season of family therapy. I remember the therapist drawing on paper and giving us permission to be angry, I remember watching my sisters' faces and wanting to protect them, and I remember how many people I hated.

Rage festered, multiplied, and spread into my soul like a cancer. I graduated from high school, enrolled in summer classes, and left for college two months early just to get away from it all. The ground under my feet was shaky; I felt as though I belonged to my anger. I knew it was time to work through the events of the past year, so halfway through my freshman year in college I decided to see a therapist. And I was scared to death.

Family therapy hadn't been optional, nor was it my decision, but this time I made the choice. Still, I was afraid of what people might think if they knew how angry and bitter I had become. I attended a Christian college where everyone was full of faith and seemed to have it all together. I didn't know anyone else who saw a counselor, and I felt a deep sense of shame for not being able to get better on my own. Far deeper than that, I was worried that something in me was broken beyond repair; I was scared at what I might discover if I peeled back the layers and examined myself more closely. Making that first painful decision to be honest about my condition and seek help was the beginning of my life-changing journey toward wholeness, but it wasn't easy. To this day, it's one of the hardest decisions I've made in my life.

The university's graduate school counseling program was housed in the Student Activity Center. It was in the same giant building as the swimming pool, rock-climbing wall, and state-of-the-art fitness center. Happy, active people with endorphins were everywhere. This seemed like a serious lack of forethought on the counseling center's part.

I walked into the office with my head down, praying no one would see me. A young grad student handed me a stack of papers and told me to take as long as I needed to fill out the forms. Through the windows in the lobby I could see rock-climbing enthusiasts scaling the walls. They high-fived each other at the top while I attempted to fill out the intake forms.

Had I attempted to hurt myself or someone else? No.

Did I hear other people's voices when there was no one else in the room? No. Well, not always.

Was I depressed? No.

Any unusual thought patterns? *Does this include obsessively planning escape routes in case of robbery, fire, or alien invasion?* I wondered.

Did I ever feel out of control? Dizzy? Headaches? Fits of rage or agitation? Yes. Yes. Yes. Yes.

Did I finish projects? Was it easy to focus? Could I multitask? No. No. No.

Tears stung my eyes. I was mortified to answer the questions and terrified to realize how many yeses I was circling. There was more going on inside of me than anger; I just didn't have words for it until I attempted to fill out the questionnaire. Answering those questions opened my eyes to holes inside of me that had always been there but had never been named. It was as if a veil was lifted and I finally saw that I had been walking through life with limps. Sitting in the counselor's office as a young eighteen-year-old girl, I felt like a failure. I did not yet know that being pro-life meant championing my *own* life. I did not know that the bravest people went to counseling and exposed their grief, anger, confusion, and pain to another person because they wanted to be well.

I've heard a myriad of convincing and not-so-convincing reasons why people don't want to see a counselor. They don't need one because they have God; they are smarter than the therapist; they wouldn't know what issue to begin with; they don't want to rehash the past; or they are afraid of what they might discover, to name a few. Unfortunately, money is also an issue for many people. But I am encouraged by the uprising of churches that have made Christian counseling services available to their congregants at reduced rates, and generous private donors within the church who make counseling possible for people in need of healing.

Besides financial issues, pride and fear seem to be at the core of many people's aversion to meeting with a therapist. And a general uncertainty about what to expect. I have found that a counselor's job is not to cast blame, induce shame, or be a self-help talking head. And their job is certainly not to replace Jesus, from whom all healing is imagined and brought forth. The role of a Christian therapist is, in part, to listen and guide their clients to see more clearly. It is a process of self-discovery and application, a journey toward the wholeness that God intended for us to possess in the first place.

We must be willing to set down the pride of having it all together and the fear of self-discovery if we are to honestly face ourselves and be made well. Are you willing to take an honest assessment of yourself? This may require meeting with a gracious guide who is trained and willing to shine a light on those places that are hard, if not impossible, to see and name on your own. Naming our broken bits is the first step to finding healing for them. Inviting someone else into your journey might be your bravest decision. No one tells you that healing is holy work when you are avoiding eye contact in the counselor's office—but it is. God uses a myriad of people in our lives to lead us back to Him; counselors are just some of them.

You Need Your Insulin

After I graduated from college and moved to Dallas, I spent a lot of time in therapy with a lady named Aggie. She was in her early seventies and had the softest, kindest eyes and fierce strength to boot. Aggie was dry and witty, compassionate and deeply empathetic, and most importantly a long lover of Jesus. Her definition of healthy was to be a fully functioning follower of Jesus Christ. She spoke the words often and assured me that I wasn't fully functioning yet! She was right. Aggie was the first person who told me my holes weren't going to go away on their own and gently suggested I needed medicine for my brain in the same way a diabetic needs insulin. I refused.

I didn't want the stigma that came with being a person who had mental illness, and I was afraid of the medicine. Horror stories played through my mind. I was convinced I would become addicted, lose my personality and sense of self, or end up on some sort of government database that targeted me for human experiments. Beyond those *completely* reasonable fears, what did it say about my relationship with Jesus if I could not pray away my mental illness? Since it was all in my head, shouldn't I be able to get control of it if I prayed hard enough, ate the right foods, did yoga, and was an all-around better person? Surely God would deliver me from this. I was embarrassed and afraid and didn't feel prepared to tackle people's lack of understanding as it pertained to my seeking psychiatric help. So for two years I refused to do the very thing I knew might bring me life: walk through the door of a psychiatrist's office.

Month after month we met, and Aggie reminded me with a laugh that God does some of his best healing work through insulin, Lipitor, chemo, and Zoloft. Each week she cracked open the National Institute of Mental Health manual and gently read the definitions that applied to my diagnosis: anxiety, obsessive-compulsive disorder, ADHD. And each week more and more of my childhood and teenage years began to make sense.

As a little girl, I knew how many times the blade of the fan swooshed over my head at night, and I could tell you the exact rhythm of the refrigerator hum. I got migraines in crowded places where I was overstimulated, like at the mall or at Six Flags amusement park. I started projects with a hyperactive wave of fervor, only to fizzle out and become completely exhausted, bored, or forgetful of the fact that I had even started a project in the first place. As a preschooler I was so distracted my parents say I walked straight into trees, walls, and parked cars. It happened so often that they finally brought me to a doctor to see if there was something wrong with my eyes! I froze while taking tests, never finished reading a single book, and started making consistent Cs by the end of sixth grade. I had an impeccable memory (to overcompensate for everything else), a fiercely active imagination, and a constant battle with unwanted, repetitive thoughts. My mind was a minefield.

As I talked to this wise woman, she asked me to pray for healing but reminded me that God brings healing in many ways. Medicine wasn't the only means and wasn't for everyone, but it might be for me. Either way, I wouldn't know unless I asked God to confirm what the different therapists had been saying since college. God would help me know what to do, she said. And that might sound altogether crazy to a nominally religious, nonspiritual person. But to me, it made perfect sense because I try to listen for God's voice speaking into every area of my life.

Some followers of Christ throw out the direction of doctors and the healing power of modern medicine because they insist God will heal them, while others go on the sole knowledge, opinion, and authority of doctors—but I believe they can work together. I can pick doctors who are respected for their skills and at the same time ask for God's confirmation, discernment, and wisdom. So I began to pray for discernment and confirmation. Were the counselors right? Was I sick? Could a psychiatrist prescribe medicine that would work powerfully and succinctly on my path toward wellness? I prayed for the right path and for peace.

I wish I could say I woke up one day and the answer was painted on a billboard surrounded by bright shiny lights with God on a megaphone. But in my own experience, God's confirmation rarely comes that way.

One morning I woke up and just knew. It wasn't a big, booming voice but a sense that it was time to be well. My prayer life, love for Jesus, exercise routine, therapy sessions, well-balanced diet, and community group were invaluable, but they alone could not treat the root cause of my sickness: those insane neurotransmitters that had been bouncing out of control for far too long. I walked into Aggie's office several days later and told her, through tears, that I thought I was ready.

"Jenny," my counselor tenderly told me, "remember, you wouldn't tell your diabetic grandmother to just pray about it, you would give her the insulin her body needs." Tears dripped down my chin as she continued to rally behind me. "Your body needs its own type of insulin. If you wouldn't deny that to a diabetic, or chemo to a friend with cancer, why would you deny proper medicine to someone whose mind needs it? This is a brave step toward being a fully functioning follower of Jesus Christ, and I'm proud of you."

I left her office and called the psychiatrist. They could see me the following week.

Oh, the Places You'll Go!

The hardest part about walking into a psychiatrist's office is that you swore you would *never* walk into a psychiatrist's office. Every bad movie you have ever seen with straitjackets and naked lunatics running through dimly lit, zombie-esque psych wards starts playing through your head.

No one wants to be seen at the psychiatrist's office. You walk into an ob-gyn's office and people are chatty. You tell the pregnant lady next to you that she looks fabulous, and she tells you it's her first child, and you talk about motherhood. There is a chance you will swap nipple cream suggestions and breast-feeding secrets with a complete stranger! You walk into a cancer center and swap chemo war stories and your opinion on wearing a wig. Waiting in the dentist's office, you might casually talk to the person across from you about your dislike of getting your teeth cleaned or that crown you *know* you are going to have to get. But you walk into a psychiatrist's office and, trust me, you don't swap hearing-voices-in-your-head stories. You sign in, keep your head down, and avoid eye contact.

Under normal circumstances, I will literally talk to a brick wall. But at the psychiatrist's office, I talk to no one. And this is part of the problem of being made well if you are suffering from a mental illness. Somehow it is okay for people to know we need dental crowns or dialysis, but drugs for obsessive-compulsive thoughts is completely different. We are uncomfortable with this type of sickness. And as long as it stays in the dark and people live in shame as they sit in their psychiatrist's office, healing will never be fully available to us. Shame is our enemy.

I took my first pill without my husband knowing when I did. It was part of a game I devised. Still terrified of the physical effects medicine might have on me and dragging my feet—I'm a wee bit hardheaded—I decided to wait a few days before taking the first of the pills. Here's how the game would work. I would start with the ADHD medicine and take it on a random day. If Ryan could tell in a positive way that I had taken the medicine, I promised to take it a second day, and possibly a third. If there was no noticeable change, or a negative change, I was out. It was a one-and-done approach, which no one else should follow—ever.

Finding the right medicine for mental illness is like learning to dance with a new partner. First you cycle through twenty partners who will absolutely not work. And they are almost enough to cause you to give up and never ever dance again. But then you find the right one, and you step on each other's toes a few thousand times until you eventually line up. And it's absolutely exhausting. Until one day you realize you are dancing beautifully together, without effort. You feel fully alive and wonder why you didn't dance together sooner.

We were in Nashville recording an album when I woke up ready to give the medicine a try. We were recording drums that day, which is like slow, repetitive torture for someone with a brain like mine. Sometimes the snare drum makes me want to kill baby animals or bang my head against a wall. Both unacceptable options. I was reading *The Time Traveler's Wife*, so I grabbed my book and headed to the front porch of the studio, which faced a busy road. As cars whirred by and drums played over and over and over again, I sat on the rocking chair and cried my way through the most beautiful love story I had ever read.

Four hours later Ryan came outside and said, "Jen, do you know what just happened?"

"What?" I asked, startled from my reading trance.

"You just sat in one place for four hours. You just finished the first book I have ever seen you finish. If this is what the medicine does for you, this is a miracle."

I took the pills the next day and then the next. Then I added in Zoloft for my OCD and anxiety. And for ten years, I faithfully took both pills.

Sometimes getting well looks like doing the thing we never thought we'd do and going places we never thought we'd go. Taking the pills that those *other* people take. Sitting in the counselor's chair, the psychiatrist's office, or the pastor's study confessing the not-well places in your body, mind, and soul is holy work.

For ten years I faithfully went to the psychiatrist because I was not well and I needed my form of insulin. I fought feeling crazy and wanting to run the other way. I fought the voice that tried to convince me there was a more dignified or holy way toward healing for a person of faith. As if the gifts and knowledge of men and medicine are shameful. "Your faith," Aggie said, "is what gives you the courage to walk through those doors, meet the doctors, and take the medicines that will make you well."

Each visit became easier, and my life was markedly different. Taking medicine became the brave, hard, holy work that I needed to submit myself to in order to experience healing. So I kept shutting out the shame and showing up. Zoloft saved my life on more than one occasion, and I will never be ashamed of that.

One morning when I woke up, just as sure as the whispers of confirmation had gently guided me into taking the medicine, they guided me back out. I had felt for some time that I no longer needed the medicine because my symptoms had greatly diminished and I found coping mechanisms that drastically reduced the duration of my episodes. But working alongside my doctor to slowly wean myself off the medicine was scary. I was afraid of having withdrawal and wondered if it was really time; I had prepared myself to take medicine indefinitely. Slow and steady I made the transition and found that I was ready and able (albeit a bit wobbly in the first few months) to live without it on the other side.

Every week I take stock of my life now and ask, am I a fully functioning follower of Jesus Christ? If not, what might lead me back to the hands of healing? Right now it looks like discipline; commitment to a small, life-giving community of people who challenge me; balance; joy; and really good breathing exercises when the chaos of my obsessive-compulsive disorder or ADHD grows loud and unruly in my mind. Maybe one day it will once again look like medicine. Or a new season of counseling, Celebrate Recovery, or perhaps a healing retreat. Whatever form healing comes in, I know I am brave enough now to step into the hard and vulnerable work it may require. I am not afraid to face myself anymore. I am ready to dance.

Healing Hurts

When I was a little girl, I collected my scabs. And sometimes . . . *I ate them.*

I'm not sure if this makes me a cannibal, or if you can be considered a cannibal for eating something that comes off your *own* body. Either way, it's disgusting and I am ashamed. Why couldn't I eat boogers like a normal child? Why didn't I save things like acorns and twigs in my ballerina jewelry box? Why scabs? These are questions I cannot answer. I have no idea what a forensic psychologist might predict as a possible outcome for a child who carefully collects scabs and sometimes eats them. But I have successfully reached thirty-five years of age without being arrested or harming baby animals, so I think, all in all, my life has turned out just fine.

I hate scabs. They are achy and dark and completely in the way. Scabs are constant reminders of some form of pain I have endured. Like tripping and skidding across the asphalt in the middle of a childhood race, or elbows dragged along my grand-parents' shag carpet during a game with my sisters. Those thick, crusty human bandages getting stuck on my Sunday stockings were perpetually with me in my childhood, drawing attention to my clumsiness. And the thing about scabs is they are in no hurry to go away. I swear there was one scab with me through the entire first grade.

As a child, I resented all they represented and willed myself to get rid of them. It was always a serious undertaking, which required one good fingernail, two napkins, a Band-Aid, and my ballerina jewelry box. Starting at the outer edge and slowly working around the circumference, I began to carefully peel the slab off, watching the reddest blood rise to the surface and run its course down my arm or leg. I thought getting rid of the scab would make it all go way. When you are six, you don't understand that healing requires time. And that it's often un-comfortable. Scabs meant my body was doing the hard work of healing, and peeling off that miraculous human bandage the body so instinctively, beautifully knew how to grow reverted the healing process back to square one. I needed scabs, ugly and obtrusive as they were. I just didn't know it yet.

It's Just Hard

I once wrote a blog about healing and the work it requires to name, treat, and follow through on the daily practices that lead toward wholeness. One woman responded, "That was depressing and exhausting to read. No one tells you the truth about that stuff." My heart hurt for her. Healing is *absolutely* exhausting. And if no one ever tells you that, then facing a healing journey could certainly be depressing.

Some people stay unwell because they don't like pain. When they get up close and stare healing in the face, they realize it hurts too bad to be made well. I understand. I despise pain. If you have no one telling you that you can do it, no one holding your hand, no one pushing you to conquer the hardest moments, the temptation to give up on healing becomes far too easy. As Becca Stevens says, "Healing is not a commodity one person gives another. It's a grace that washes over us. It's not magical. It's just hard."[1]

I sat next to a woman on a flight recently who had been in a life-altering car wreck. The doctors are still baffled that she lived through it. She wore a neck brace that connected to another brace, which held together her entire upper body. She had been driving home when she assumes she glanced down at her phone, hit a brick mailbox, and flipped her car. She rolled five times down an embankment, was ejected from her car, and landed smack-dab between two trees in a patch of nasty poison ivy. "Of course I landed in poison ivy!" She said when the property owner found her, she was still buckled into her seat; the entire chair had been ejected. She laughed at the tragic irony of it all. "Now my job is just healing, and that's a full-time job."

I admired her so much. She knew the road ahead of her was long and painful, but she was grateful for the chance to do the hard work of healing, because it meant living.

Talk to the doctors, nurses, and patients in a burn unit, a traumatic brain-injury ward, or the people coming back from war without the arms and legs they went to war with—they know best the hard work of healing. The girls to whom I dedicate this book—survivors of human trafficking and the most depraved acts of sexual violence—will echo the same sentiments. Healing is hard.

One sweet sister wrote me recently and said,

> *Really having a rough day. Counseling was intense, my heart hurts, and anger seems to be the only thing that makes it feel better. I feel literally sick to my stomach. The past hurts, looking at it hurts, picking it up and dealing with it hurts. I am weary today. Could use all the prayers I can get.*

Her healing journey requires she process, grieve, and work through past sexual abuse and exploitation at the hands of her father. Weariness often washes over her in this journey.

I responded,

> *Praying for you as you fall asleep tonight. You are never ever alone. Even in this. You are fighting for a NEW future, and sometimes that means fighting the demons of the past, putting them in their place and putting them to rest. Though it may take a battle, they will not beat you. You can do this.*
>
> *I am praying specifically tonight for you to feel the intense, calming, restful love of Christ. I pray you might let the anger run its course and then, when it is gone and you are drained of it, you will collapse in the arms of Jesus and feel Him whispering His LOVE and peace over you. I pray He gives you rest. Just rest. Set the past down for a bit. Focus on today or just look at Jesus . . . He will know exactly how to care for you. You are loved and not alone. I am lifting you up tonight. I am SO proud of you. You are walking a hard road and doing holy work. Do not give up, sweet girl.*

She wrote back the next day.

A good night's sleep helped a lot. Just putting one foot in front of the other and doing the best I can. I never knew going through healing could be so hard. It takes so much, but I know God is there. I sincerely appreciate your prayers and support. Much love to you.

It Takes Time

My daughter Annie recently got her first scab, and I was relieved to find she was not even remotely tempted to eat it. But she did confide in me that it felt weird and achy and she was going to peel it off because she was totally grossed out by it. I told her all about scabs and how I collected them when I was her age (though I omitted telling her about the eating part). We talked about how remarkable the body is, that it instinctively knows how to get better when we are sick or hurt. I made her pinky promise she would not take the scab off, because she needed the scab while the wound was healing. She seemed to understand the whole process, and after locking pinkies with me she said, "Mom, healing hurts and I hate it!"

Truer words have never been spoken. Some people give up on their healing before they even get started. They peel the scab off, and when it grows back, they peel it off again. It's a perpetual cycle that never allows them to move into the next phase. Once the wound is finally covered by a scab, you must sit on your hands long enough so as not to prematurely peel it off. And then? Prepare for the long haul. Because odds are healing is going to take a while.

At one point in my counseling journey, my therapist asked me to write about a traumatic moment I experienced as a thirteen-year-old that made me very afraid for my life. "Go back there," he said. "Write everything. What were you wearing? What was said? What happened? What would you tell the little girl in that exact moment?"

I went to a coffee shop after our session and attempted to write about the incident. It was so painful to revisit that I instantaneously began to exhibit signs of a full-blown panic attack. I tried a few days later and then again a few days after that. Each time I would begin to shake and feel as though I couldn't breathe and I might pass out. At the next session I told my counselor it was impossible. I could not go back there and I did not want to.

"You must go back there and tell that little girl she does not have to live in fear anymore. That she is going to be okay," he said. It took three months before I was able to revisit that painful moment from my past and tell that little girl she was going to live and she didn't have to be afraid. I told her through heaving sobs and cried for three days straight. God has restored my sense of safety, but it did not happen overnight as a result of one prayer or one counseling session. It took three months before I could even go back to that place—for some it takes three years, or thirty. The miracle of healing in that situation looked less like an immediate result and more like a tearstained journal, a good therapist, antianxiety medicine, and a God who met me in my fear and reminded me of my safety.

Everything in me wants to tell you this: That the wounds are all going to go away painlessly, in your sleep. That if you pray, forgive, take a pill, believe in God's ability to perform miracles, and get a good night's sleep, you will wake up tomorrow morning healed. Everything in me wants that to be true for us—healing that comes without a cost. Without the scabs and scars. And sometimes God miraculously redeems, restores, and heals in divine ways that seemingly *do* occur overnight. Sometimes we touch the hem of Jesus' garment, like the bleeding woman did, and healing happens immediately.[2] But most of my healing hasn't happened in an instant. I touch the hem of Jesus' garment and know He is present and with me as I walk through the brokenness. His healing power carries my fragments, and little by little I am slowly mended back together.

The hard work of healing is always with me; it rarely comes easily and often hurts. It might require unearthing the past only to lay it to rest; experimenting with medicines until your body finds the type it can tolerate (all the while dragging your mind and body through the mud); leaning into mental, physical, and spiritual disciplines that bring you one step closer to wholeness; and a daily decision to keep fighting. In the same way one healthy meal, hard workout, or lap-band surgery will not ensure health indefinitely, one pill, counseling session, or season of mental wellness will not carry a person for a lifetime. If a diabetic has to watch their sugar and take insulin for the rest of their lives to manage the disease, why should I expect anything different with my disease? Being made well often takes time.

Sitting with Her

Several weeks after Maggie and Ellen died, I found myself sitting in my counselor's office in Nashville, tears running down my face before the session even started. He's not a traditional counselor. He's more like poet meets theologian meets a regular at the bar, *and* he happens to have all the right degrees that make him an official therapist.[3] I cried and rambled; he listened.

And then as he usually does, he searched his bookshelf for the answer that was already written. Maybe healers are not so much creators of miracles as they are pursuers of truths that already exist, buried somewhere, forgotten.

This time it was Mary Oliver and a poem on giving grief an identity, a name. He asked me if I had named my grief yet and given her proper space in my life. Then he read the words of "Love Sorrow." In the poem, grief is personified as a little girl who needs to be taken on a walk and needs her hair brushed. I immediately hated her. Whoever thought of giving grief person-hood status obviously hadn't grieved. I didn't want her to have a name or face or any presence in my life; I wanted her to go away. I didn't care if she needed her hair brushed; I wanted her to die. But I faintly smiled as he read, pretending to understand the importance of naming my grief, calling her Emily or Ann. I left wondering why I even go to counseling and what in the world he was talking about.

Several days later I was hiking when I knew she was there. I saw her run ahead on the path, invisible yet so real I could feel the air brush against me as she whizzed by. My grief was longing to be set free, but I had been ignoring her. Now she was here with me and I needed to face her.

I saw her a little ways up the trail, sitting on the bench. I sat down and stared at the spot next to me, avoiding eye contact. "Hi," I said to her with very little affection. Like a villainous stepmother, I looked her up and down as if she were not my child and I would never embrace her. Surely she knew she was unwanted.

She looked a bit like my own daughter. Six years old, un-brushed hair, skinny as a rail, and wild-eyed. I noticed she was cold and shivering. Without tenderness or permission, my heart began to bend toward her. I sat quietly, without words, and finally decided I should give her my sweater. After all, though I was not quite willing to claim her, she was somebody's little girl. I draped the sweater over her tiny shoulders. We sat a bit longer and then she stood up, looked at me, and reached out her little fingers. I accepted her invitation.

For nearly three hours we walked hand in hand. One hour in, I finally spoke. I apologized for hating her and not wanting her. "You were unexpected," I confessed. She never said a word since she was not real; she only walked without expression, holding my hand.

She was the personification of all my grief that needed permission to exist and be known. All the death and loss I had experienced found a way into her, made her up, and created her out of nothing, and then she beckoned me to care for her as I would care for my own daughter. It was a supernatural invitation to open my heart and nurture my most broken pieces. I no more wanted to deal with grief than I want to deal with taxes, yet in that moment I knew it was time to give her a name and a face and let her be real.

I watched her as we walked, and I quietly wept. Why had she entered my life, when would she leave, and how long might I be stuck caring for her?

I've had moments where I felt an out-of-body experience occurring. Moments where the rest of the world is talking, living, breathing—but I am observing it unfold from some completely *other* place. As if I have floated up to the corner of the room and am looking down, watching, detached from reality. Anyone who has experienced an episode like this can attest that it usually occurs in the midst of physical or emotional shock, in the throes of a panic attack, or in a state of spiritual rapture that causes the physical world to recede and the Holy Spirit world to come alive.

The moment in the woods was the *exact* opposite. I was fully present and as tethered to reality as possible. My hike had begun as all my hikes do. A quick call to my husband to let him know when to expect me back, a bit of stretching, eyes darting around the trail looking for deer, and a ruthless inner judge telling me to walk faster for the sake of my thighs. There was nothing particularly special about the morning my grief showed up. She made no appointment and gave me no warning. She appeared suddenly and without invitation. And I very well could have chalked it up to some sort of strange indigestion and willed myself straight past her. But I didn't, because the voice of my therapist and the poet Mary Oliver came back to me. *Have you given grief its space? Have you given her a name?* And the truth was, I hadn't.

Though I had cried many tears, they were only wild, involuntary bursts of emotion, a physical reality I had very little control over. Like goose bumps. But I had not deeply wrestled with grief. I had avoided looking her full in the eyes, afraid she may overwhelm and consume me and I would never recover. Fear kept me from facing grief. And the longer I avoided her, the further I got from healing.

Looking at her in the woods that day, tender and frail, I wondered why I had been so afraid of her. Why had I cowered from creating a compassionate space for my grief to be known and accepted? I knew all too quickly that I was guilty of being equal parts afraid and lazy. Tending to another area of my soul seemed too costly. And exhausting. Wasn't I tending to enough? Couldn't I skip grief and get straight to healing? I wanted healing that came without all the work. Healing that didn't require me to first sit with my grief and give her a name. Healing that happened at the miraculous finish line with no blood, sweat, and tears. Was that too much to ask?

"In my life, healing hasn't come free, nor has it come easily. There's always been a cost to healing," Becca Stevens says. "Healing cannot happen without scars, and those scars cost us."[4]

Most healing comes at a high cost, with great effort and intention. It looks less like a giant eraser that miraculously takes away all the pain and delivers instant restoration, and more like the slow drip of water from a faucet, filling the empty glass below drop by drop. Healing takes its time and never follows a schedule. This is maddening. If only it came as sure and steady as the hospital bills, mortgage payments, and that one person you don't want to run into but always do. Always. But it doesn't. Healing happens when you are brave enough to go into the woods with sorrow and into the counselor's office with raw tears. One tiny step after another.

I left the shade of the towering trees that day a bit more healed than when I entered them. The sting of death was not miraculously zapped away, but I was no longer afraid to look it in the eyes. When I did so, I began to render the pain powerless. I stared at the ghostly girl who held within her all my grief and realized I beheld my deep sadness and would still live to talk about it. I walked out of the woods alive.

Slow Dancing

recently took a class at my home church about the Angli-
can way of life. Before the rector jumped into Henry VIII
and the Thirty-Nine Articles, we were led through a ubiquitous
get-to-know-you game. He wanted us to go around the small
circle and say our name, what our religious upbringing was like,
our favorite book, and what a dream day to ourselves might
consist of. So I said my name and my church background, but
couldn't think of a book to save my life. Thank God they didn't
ask what my profession was. Though I have devoured and loved
many books, the pressure was just too much and I froze.

My favorite book is *Atlas Shrugged*, a 1,160-page fictional story
about the country's most brilliant thinkers, industrialists, artists,
and creators removing themselves—and their contributions—
from society and disappearing to a place where no one could

benefit from their giftedness but themselves. It's the most seductive and compelling argument for rational selfishness I have ever read. It appeals to every egotistical, base instinct a human can have. As a young twenty-year-old, I almost believed in it. Now I love the book because it masterfully represents everything I don't ever want to be—it is the complete and total opposite of my desire to follow in the footsteps of Christ. But you can't drop that into a five-second get-to-know-you game without time to properly explain why it is your favorite book and also that you aren't actually an objectivist.

I thought about *East of Eden* because it sounds so smart, but I love-hate *East of Eden* like I love-hate roller-coaster rides. I kick myself for getting on board the whole way up, hate myself the whole way down, and get off with a sense of pride that I made it through the roller coaster. That's what Steinbeck does to me. His words wreck me in the best and worst sorts of ways.

There are a slew of Christian books I could have named as well. *Embracing the Love of God*, *Abba's Child*, *The Prodigal Son*, and *Between the Dreaming and the Coming True*, to name a few. But you can't very well be the first person to throw out a laundry list of Christian books about God's love or you become *that* girl—it's like the adult version of yelling "Jesus" when the Sunday school teacher asks for an answer.

So in a moment of literary panic, I laughed and shrugged my shoulders in a way that indicated *I had never read a book in my entire life*. My inner English giant cringed. What was wrong with my brain and mouth? I quietly prayed that no one in the new church would *ever* find out I had written a book.

I followed this unimpressive non-response to the book question by blurting out that if I had a day all to myself, I would go sit on a rock. Everyone laughed and I immediately regretted this answer. Although it was true, I berated myself for the inability to produce a single answer that did not make me sound like a complete buffoon. I tried to explain that there was a *particular* rock in a river nestled in the foothills of a mountain in New Mexico that absolutely stole my heart. But it didn't matter much. I was the Southern church girl who didn't read books and would spend my one day of perfection on a rock. Bless her heart.

Here's what I meant to say: I would go sit on this *one* rock in the Santa Fe River, let the water wash over my toes—and my soul—and walk away well. Because that one river, the way it bends around the mountain and makes me feel like I can touch the sky, always makes me well. Oh, and *Atlas Shrugged*.

All the Places

It helps to know the places where you most come alive, experience peace, and know healing. If you're given the chance to travel there, or tell a group of strangers about it at church, it's nice to have it tucked away in your back pocket. And believe me, I've got a list. I'm an outdoors girl. There's the river in New Mexico and the stretch of beach at Crystal Cove State Park and the trail buried deep in the woods surrounding Mount Rainier. There's the bay on Anna Maria Island and the dock in Belize overlooking the turquoise water and that one house on the lake in Minnesota. This is just the beginning of a long list of places I have traveled and found some measure of healing.

On top of the places I have already grown to love, I have a dream list of far-flung locations I am convinced would mend anyone. Fiji is where *all* healing should happen, in my personal opinion. If you can't be healed with the balmy South Pacific breeze blowing through your hair, on a hammock overlooking the baby-blue water, where *can* you be healed? Left to my own devices, I would declare that all mankind be healed on the islands of Fiji with our toes sunk deep into the warm waters of the South Pacific Ocean. Mind you, I've never been, but deep down I have a feeling it's my kind of place.

Then, like Elizabeth Gilbert, we would eat, pray, and love our way through Italy, Bali, and India and find our healing on long pilgrimages to exotic destinations. So many people are healed in fascinating locations as they pedal their bikes across a continent, scale scary mountains, hibernate with wolves, and do whatever else they do on those insane *National Geographic* reality shows.

After all that, we would head to a monastery. Entire books are centered on the weeks, months, and years pilgrims have silently spent in monasteries seeking life transformation. They have visions, lose a lot of weight, go into prayer trances, and leave with theology-shaking, world-changing experiences. Or at least a quiet peace in their souls that I can't always seem to find in my living room.

Sometimes getting away, if even for a single night to a hotel down the street (or a friend's guest bedroom!), is the best medicine. But it can't be the only medicine. And I wonder how long healing that happens in fantastical ways actually lasts. The beach is good for my soul, and I experience immense healing when my feet are dug deep into the sand. But then I go home and the sand eventually washes off, and I find the holes—though smaller in size—are still right where I left them. They just have a suntan.

Don't get me wrong; not all healing takes time, and plenty of long-term mending happens when one removes themselves from the ordinary and intentionally seeks to be made well in the unordinary. I don't doubt for one minute that Jesus makes people well on their extravagant pilgrimages to find freedom, but sometimes I wonder how He makes normal people well. Those of us who can't afford physically, monetarily, or for some other reason to traipse the globe in search of what we are missing. If you can't check your obligations at the door and leave behind your spouse, children, friends, job, pet, or other responsibilities in order to chase healing to the farthest corners of the earth, can it still be found?

Be Where You Are

When I first started cowriting songs with well-established Nashville musicians, I was amazed at their dedication to the craft. I had never taken a voice lesson or been taught how to write a song. I did it out of untrained instinct. Back then, in order for me to conjure up a song out of thin air, I had a list of things I needed first. Not green M&M's, water served at seventy-two degrees, or other high-maintenance requests like that. But, I needed to be in the right sort of mood. Preferably in a room with sunlight, in the morning or late at night, after a hearty meal, and it helped if I had just walked through some sort of drama or epiphany in my life. Those were my standards for songwriting. I didn't know how to write a song unless I was inspired and the ambience was on point.

The first man I cowrote with was a legend in the Christian music industry. I remember walking into his writing studio at the publishing house, nervous and afraid. It was a sterile environment with bright fluorescent lights in the middle of the afternoon. Who wrote songs at 2:00 p.m.? I didn't know the first thing about this man, and there was nothing in particular weighing on my heart. How in the world was I going to be able to—*poof*—write a song?

I noticed a quote that was printed and taped to his piano. "The great composer does not set to work because he is inspired, but becomes inspired because he is working." When I asked him about the quote, he quietly said that this was the mantra he lived by, and it was very likely the reason he had written more chart-topping songs in the past twenty years than he ever dreamed he could. If he waited for inspiration, he may never write a song. Instead, he endeavored to show up for work each day and trusted that inspiration would visit him on occasion. He taught me a lot about songwriting that day—and also about healing.

If my healing is dependent on that one rock in Santa Fe, I'm in trouble. As much as I love that rock, it's been nearly three years since I've been back. Of course an amazing massage, my toes dug deep into the sand at the foot of the ocean, and sitting beside my favorite river are my first choices when I am longing for restoration, but they cannot be the only places I turn to, and I must remind myself they are only starting points.

If we put pressure on one single place, experience, or event to heal us, we run the risk of having our expectations greatly dashed and shortchanging the healing that can happen in our everyday lives. The kind that comes slowly and faithfully, in the ordinary moments. "The journey to healing is usually not fast—it's a slow dance," Becca Stevens says. "My healing journey has taken thousands of prayers, countless small bites of bread, and gallons of wine one sip at a time."[1] A lifetime of communion, she says, each sacrament leading her one step closer and one step closer. Most of the time healing looks like a slow dance, not an epic trip around the globe.

In the same way one would not expect a weekend marriage conference to ensure the health of a marriage for a lifetime, one should not expect to take a healing trek through Machu Picchu and be made well indefinitely. Once-in-a-lifetime healing experiences can bring about extraordinary change in a person's soul, but it is not the be-all, end-all of healing and wholeness. Being made well happens over the course of a lifetime. So unless you are committed to hiking Machu Picchu periodically throughout the entirety of your life, you will need to tap into healing that can happen wherever you are.

It is in the midst of our ordinary, everyday lives that we are to be made well. We raise children and grow up in our marriages. Volunteer in churches, schools, and community organizations. Take care of aging parents. Study, prepare, and search for the perfect career. And with what we have left, we try to grow into the community around us. We are known to take a few weeks of vacation each year (if we actually take them), but a week away in Gulf Shores or Hawaii or the mountains is a far cry from a pilgrimage to be made well. Dragging kids through Disney World doesn't qualify as a healing pilgrimage either. You actually need to work in *extra* healing after a trip to Disney with young children.

The reality is, many of us will never traipse the world for months on end indulging in new sights, sounds, and sunsets in order to obtain much-needed healing. That type of luxury lives far beyond the reach of regular lives. Where then do we turn for healing in the ebb and flow of our everyday existence? Can healing happen between breakfast and babies, between lunch breaks and long lines, between raising children and rising careers, between momentous occasions and mundane living? I think so.

Every Day Made Well

I go hiking most mornings after dropping Annie off at school. It takes exactly four minutes to drive to Radnor Lake from the front door of her school, and if ever I am going to get physical activity worked into my daily life, mornings are my chance. It's an added bonus that I don't have to pay for a gym membership here, and it's absolutely beautiful. But I fight going the same way I fight brushing my teeth each night. It is absolutely mind-boggling to me that I still feel devastating dread each time I have to brush my teeth, but I *do*. Some of Ryan's and my biggest fights have to do with ultimatums regarding the brushing of my teeth and washing of my body. These feel like such unnecessary burdens on my life. I have exerted all my energy on being human and adulting. Must I really brush my teeth and shower as well? Ryan says I am trapped in a nine-year-old boy's body.

But I push through the resistance, brushing my teeth and hiking and being grown-up in as many ways as possible. And what I find on the other side is my completely bewildered self. Why haven't I enjoyed this all along? I do like clean teeth and clean hair! I do like the woods! While I've been sitting around feeling sorry for myself as I watch the Facebook feeds of other people's amazing trips around the world—there were woods four minutes away filled with beauty and wonder. Invitation extended. Waiting for me to push through my resistance and come.

Now the longer I linger in these woods, the more acutely attuned I am to the rustle of leaves beneath a chipmunk or a squirrel, beneath a fawn and its mother. I have begun to name the trees and classify the leaves. I know which branch the barn owl likes to perch on.

Lately this certain hiking trail is exactly where I wander to be still and soak in God's glory. I am grateful for the meandering path and a particular patch of lavender-colored flowers and the momma deer and her babies I encounter each morning. I am mindful of the leaves, the wind, and the ever-changing colors of the landscape. I sit in silence. Here in these sacred pauses, I can't help but be made new, little by little. I get the feeling I belong here and some of my best healing work can be accomplished on the hiking trails in my own backyard.

My thirty-fifth birthday was relatively simple. No friends came over to celebrate; it was just Ryan, Annie, and me. My favorites. Ryan cooked chicken spaghetti because I love ooey-gooey Southern casseroles. We met over a pan of chicken spaghetti in college. (Apparently, I didn't just go back for seconds, I went back for thirds too. And he was hooked.) So it has always been my favorite.

The two of them do birthdays up right. For several days they had been giving me cards and taking me to dinner. Ryan even surprised me with concert tickets the week before to go see one of my favorite musicians play at the Ryman Auditorium. On the morning of my birthday, Annie sprang out of bed, dressed herself without my nagging, and came to the living room beaming with pride because of her helpfulness. After school she secretly decorated my birthday cake with an abundance of bright pink sprinkles and couldn't wait to give me my present: a handmade card that said, "I am so excited it is your 35 BIRTHDAY." Ryan had a few other gifts for me, which totally took me by surprise, and the two of them sang "Happy Birthday" as the candles flickered in the quiet dark around our kitchen table.

After dinner Annie said her real present was a performance. She ran to her room and emerged in a soft pink ballet outfit. The cat snuggled down into my lap. The classical music began. Annie quietly danced around the room, her face and body freely following the beauty of the melodies. She didn't learn these moves in a dance class and had never heard the songs before. She just asked her dad to play classical music and moved as her heart was led. Her sensitive soul rises and falls with the music she hears; her countenance changes with each new note.

Watching Annie dance is like watching a swan glide over water, watching rain roll off a rose petal after a storm. It is effortless and intense, peaceful and powerful. As she danced and her daddy smiled and the cat purred in my lap, I recognized a peace settling deep within me, filling a hole. I wasn't on my favorite rock and was nowhere near the ocean, but wave after wave of gratitude and peace washed over me, and I knew in that tiny, unadorned moment I was being made well.

Where do you go to be made well? To breathe deeply, listen for God's voice, and know His peace? I used to think this could only happen with a Bible in hand, wrestling over Scripture verses, or on an exotic trip. But now I know if my eyes are open, I experience peace that passes understanding in a myriad of places. Most of which I can experience in my own living room as my baby girl dances the night away. Or in my backyard as I watch the sun rise and fall each new day. Or on that one trail four minutes from my daughter's school. Sure, the ocean is great too. Miraculous transformations on exotic, far-flung journeys are dreamy. But most of life happens in my living room, where a thousand tiny moments cobbled together look like healing. It's no quick fix. But I prefer slow dancing anyway.

Interlude

Sparrows

ealing doesn't always come right away, or right on time for that matter. It certainly doesn't always show up in big, flashy brushstrokes like front-row concert tickets. But sometimes it does. The important thing is to keep your eyes and heart open, knowing that healing avenues are at work all around you; they belong to you if you claim them. When we begin to live with a holy awareness, believing that God is at work around us, we unlock a wealth of healing at our fingertips. Simple treasures in creation and the everyday kindness of another person can serve as healing balms. The best prayer I can pray is "May I live with holy awareness."

Several weeks after my nieces died, I was hiking when a ginormous walnut fell from a towering tree above and knocked me square on the head. The impact was so hard and I was so startled that I actually fell to the ground! I quickly got up, looked around, and hoped no one had seen a walnut take me out. A knot formed on the top of my head almost instantly and throbbed. I contemplated whether I needed to turn around and head back home because *I probably had a concussion.* But something within beckoned me to stay and challenged me to push through the pain, which is *not* a common practice in my life. I despise pain and rarely push through it, but that day I did.

As I walked, head throbbing, I went a little more slowly than I normally would and sat on more benches along the way. Nothing spectacular happened. I saw a few deer and an owl, but mostly I just walked. And as I moved forward I became aware of the beating of my heart, maybe because it was in tempo with the throbbing of my head. So steady and calm was she—my brave heart. She had been doing her job quietly and faithfully all along. I was so overwhelmed with gratitude for my heart that tears fell down my cheeks and I began to thank her out loud. I thanked her for beating on no matter what was happening in my life. For being constant. For marching forward during those past six months when I was sure I would fold.

Healing is not as complicated as we like to make it. The steadfastness of our own hearts is enough to give us pause and mend us in tiny ways if we allow it to. Becca Stevens says, "When you pick a blackberry straight from the bush and eat it, you can feel the healing."[1]

I once met a woman dying of cancer at a military hospital in Washington State. She shuffled into the hospital's chapel, frail, bald, and connected to her IV treatment bags. A surgical mask covered her face. She beamed. Life oozed out of her in a sobering and beautiful way as she sang along to songs like "Great Is Thy Faithfulness" and "Amazing Grace."

Anne Lamott says the last thing you want to do if you are feeling pathetic about yourself is hang out with dying people:

> They will ruin everything for you.
>
> First of all, friends like this may not even think of themselves as dying, although they clearly are, according to recent scans and gentle doctors' reports. But no, they see themselves as fully alive. They are living and doing as much as they can, as well as they can, for as long as they can. . . .
>
> They bust you by being grateful for the day, while you are obsessed with how thin your lashes have become and how wide your bottom.[2]

Barb was like this. Though she was dying, she was fully alive. And grateful for everything.

In particular, she wanted to tell me about the sparrow God sent her. Every day she spent time outside because there was no sense in living if you couldn't. I gather that's how most people feel who live in the Pacific Northwest; the majesty of the mountains and the ocean never lost their luster for her. Her oncology nurse would wheel her outside each afternoon to soak in as much nature as she could. One day while she sat in her usual spot at the patio table, a sparrow flew down and perched right in front of her. Without flinching, Barb stuck her finger out and the sparrow jumped on! The next day she went outside and the sparrow reappeared, again jumping onto her finger when she extended it. This continued day after day for months on end.

"My God told me, 'Barbara, if I care for the sparrows, how much more will I care for you?'" she said. "He sends me that little sparrow every day to remind me how much He cares for me. I am so loved." She wondered, if she could get clearance and was able to leave the hospital that night to attend my concert, would I be able to sing "His Eye Is on the Sparrow" for her?

When I saw her walk through the door that evening, I wept. We sang her song that night, and to watch her sing along would leave the hardest heart softened. She just kept fighting for life, living well, and basking in God's love, which washed over her in wave after wave.

Weeks after the show I received a package from her. A Willow Tree statue of a lady with arms outstretched and sparrows perched on them. And a picture of her frail finger with the tiniest bird perched on it.

If He cares for the sparrows, how much more will He care for you?

> *With all my love,*
> *Barb*

Several weeks later I received a letter from her nurse.

Jenny, Barb went to heaven yesterday morning while at her friend's house. They had been best friends and sisters in Christ from Barb's Air Force days (she was retired from the Air Force), and her plan was to be at her friend's house when "the time came." So she was surrounded by her "family," and after a prayer she smiled at them and then fell asleep.

I don't know if Barb told you much about her life, but her parents were alcoholics and she was raised in foster homes. I always admired her for breaking that cycle, graduating from nursing school, and going into the military. She had a strong faith in our Lord, and I thought how appropriate that she would pass away on the most beautiful day we have had in the Pacific

Northwest this year, AND on Easter. As we celebrate the resurrection of our Lord and Savior today, we also celebrate Barb's transition to being with Jesus.

What a way to go home. Barb taught me that the smallest things in the natural world, as tiny as a sparrow, have the power to draw me near to God's love for me. "One of the great wonders of creation is that God uses our natural world to alert us to his presence," Margaret Feinberg says.[3] It's not complicated. If my eyes are open and I am looking, I will see that the whole world is full of tiny particles of healing pointing me back to the Healer.

9

Living with Limps

To be quite honest, I was terrified of Thanksgiving the year my family experienced so many deaths. Holidays are typically stressful in the best and worst ways. Schedules, road trips, different beds, tired kids, unusual routines, faces you love but haven't lived with since high school, and about ten extra people squeezed into houses built for, well, not ten. Most people walk into the holidays silently praying that no one turns on the wrong cable news channel or brings up politics, hoping that they don't get caught giving the stink eye to another sibling's kid, and praying that everyone eats the food with as much enthusiastic joy as the hostess is hoping for.

It would be our biggest Thanksgiving feast in years. Three sisters, four nieces, three husbands, one tiny house, two excited grandparents, one great-grandma, and more food than we could stomach. There would be the normal aforementioned family issues that people face while heading into the holidays. Joy and stress commingling. Fault lines shifting. Families colliding. But this time there would be fresh new holes and deep grief. Missing spots at the table. This year there would be no Grandpa. No Mamaw. No Maggie. No Ellen.

I was worried that although our family had weathered the most immediate moments of our deep losses, we would come together, thrust into the familial chaos of holidays, and finally implode. I knew we had made it through the center of the storm. The part where you are thrashed about until your bones hurt and your soul cries mercy. But sometimes, when it's all said and done, that's the easy part. The eye of the hurricane is calm. In the eye of the storm we get these magical little chemicals called endorphins. They kick in and kick butt. At the storm's height, standing right in the center of it, you are surrounded by the prayers of people, generous doses of God's peace that passes understanding, superhuman strength from those endorphins, and an overall out-of-body sensation that keeps you from *actually* feeling the full weight of it all. If you are unfamiliar with the latter sensation, think of the out-of-body, never-ending, exhaustive blur that is the first three months of parenting a newborn. Were it not for this blurring of reality, people may not procreate *ever* again.

It's the chaos before and after the storm that wreaks havoc and brings about destruction. Waiting for the phone call, trying more drugs, juggling living people and dying people. The financial burdens that follow, the empty spot in bed, the unused nursery, the spaghetti aisle meltdowns. People who have buried will tell you these are the hardest parts—not the funeral, but what comes before and after.

I was afraid the hurricane would trigger an earthquake. And the earthquake would trigger a tsunami. That we would all show up and have meltdowns, simultaneously, in our own crazy ways around the Thanksgiving dinner table. As if all our grief, raw and unvarnished, would rub together like sandpaper until the fault lines had no choice but to finally falter.

What happened instead was quite unexpected.

We had our best Thanksgiving ever. I think it's because we all came with our limps, battle scars, and sadness, and we were kind to one another. Empathetic. Gracious. And honest.

I think it's because Ray and Sarah were brave enough to get out of bed and keep living, boldly proclaiming that though they were devastated and broken, Emmanuel was carrying them. I think it's because my eighty-three-year-old grandma who had to take her husband of fifty-five years off life support in August was brave enough to get on a plane by herself and show up for a day of giving thanks. I think it's because my dad loved on the granddaughters he *did* have, but when it came time to pray around the Thanksgiving table, he gave thanks for Maggie and Ellen too. And then he openly wept, and in so doing, gave us permission to do the same. I think it's because we played football. And wore turkey hats. And drank more Starbucks coffee than can possibly be good for us. And played dominoes. And let our girls run free. And let our tears run free. And dwelt in the beauty of the moment while also being able to say to one another, "Hey, remember that one year FROM HELL?! Yeah, it's almost over now. We're making it through after all."

And I mostly think it's because we all showed up when we didn't want to. When we didn't think we could and didn't know how to or what the outcome might be. We showed up anyway. And we all knew we were walking on fault lines that might give at any moment, but still we walked. And you know what? The fault lines seemed to realign, to pull in tight, to grow stronger under the earth beneath us. There were no stress fractures, no earthquakes, and no tremors. There was strength in showing up with what little we had, but showing up all the while.

Showing Up

We are not always gracious with one another's limps because we are unsure of what to do with them. Do we acknowledge the limp? Pretend it isn't there? Have pity? Pride? What do we say when the limp is obvious?

There was a woman at my aunt Debbie's funeral who was missing a leg. I saw my incredibly inquisitive little cousin circling her like a vulture, and before any of us could reach him, he looked her in the eyes and said loud enough for the entire funeral parlor to hear, "Hey lady, where'd your leg go?!" The adults in the room were mortified. I can't remember her response verbatim, but it was jovial and something along the lines of a shrug and a simple "I lost it!" This seemed to satisfy my toddler cousin. Yep. She lost it. Well, that settles that.

Sometimes it is hard for the well ones to show up for the limpy ones. We have so many fears. What if we go at the wrong time? What if we are intruding, or don't bring an appropriate gift, or say the wrong words? What if we accidentally blurt out, "Hey lady, where'd your leg go?!" Or worse, we burst into tears and offer nothing to the mix but our own sorrow. So often when we feel the Holy Spirit prompting us to step into someone's heartache and brokenness, we let the voices of doubt, fear, and pride rob us of the opportunity to be a part of that person's healing process. Sadly, sometimes the value of our own schedules running according to plan trumps our availability to show up for one another. How many times have we forfeited our rights as God's active agents of healing in another person's life because we talked ourselves off a ledge and remained quiet, safe, practical, on schedule, or out of the way?

I will always remember the first couple that came into Sarah's hospital room after Maggie and Ellen died. They weren't put together or perfect, and they both began to weep as soon as they walked through the doors. The wife said, "I don't even have words, sweetie. I'm so sorry. I just . . ." Her voice trailed off, and she looked down at the blue Dillard's gift box she was holding. Then she looked up. "Silk pajamas? I brought pajamas." And she quietly held the box out. It was one of the most beautiful acts of love I have ever seen.

This couple wasted no time. They didn't call ahead or worry about being in the way. They came even though they knew the best they had to offer were tears and silk pajamas. And when I stopped them at the door to warn them that the girls—tiny, lifeless babies—were still in the room, they went inside anyway and bore up under the weight of crushing grief with our family. I will never forget them.

On a previous day, as the long weeks wore on and we waited for the outcome of Sarah's pregnancy, my longtime friend Missy invited me over for breakfast and a time of prayer. Our friend Lauren joined, and after eating we moved to the couch and tried to pray, but the words were hard to come by. Missy had recently walked through the loss of her own unborn baby and knew all too well the pain we were experiencing. As the tears slipped down our cheeks, someone quietly prayed, "God, you know what we want to say and what we need to hear," but that's as far as the talking went. We sat silently with our tears, unable to find the right words, and that's when I realized the radio had been on the whole time. At that exact moment, when our words were few, one of my band's songs, "Hope Now," came on. We looked up at one another in amazement—I could not believe I was hearing my own voice on the radio.

Only God could answer our prayers in that way. My own voice washed over me. "You are my shelter from the storm, and everything rides on hope now," the words said.[1] I was deeply moved by the moment. Grateful for a God who would speak directly to my pain in such a personal way and grateful for friends who were brave enough to sit in the silence and tears, without needing to babble with tons of words. It was because of their silence that I was able to hear the radio in the first place and the small miracle of God showing up with my own words as healing agents.

There's an old country song that says, "You say it best when you say nothing at all."[2] Good healers know that words aren't always necessary and tears are okay. I thank God for the people in my life who have jumped without restraint smack-dab into the middle of my darkest night to offer up silk pajamas and silent moments.

Our Best Teachers

Learning how to show up to the party with our limps is both humbling and terrifying. It is a learning curve.

I have a friend who was born with a condition that caused him to lose vision in his right eye as a newborn, and eventually he was fitted for a prosthetic eye. The first time I met him we were minutes into the conversation when he announced, "I have a fake eyeball!" I have to admit, I was a little taken aback.

Who simply announces they have a fake eyeball? But the more I thought about it, the more impressed I was with his ability to lead with his limp instead of living in shame or embarrassment, or simply glossing over it and acting like it wasn't a part of who he was. It *is* a part of him, as all limps are. It's what you do with the limp that defines its role in your life. My friend embraces his limp—he even has a prosthetic with the North Carolina Tar Heels logo painted on it! He teaches the rest of us how to feel comfortable in acknowledging our broken bits, because he is comfortable acknowledging his.

In my experience, when we give people an opportunity to teach us how to respond to their situation, they are more than willing to do so. Anyone who has lived with their limp long enough—and does not live in bondage to it—generally has a good sense of humor about their condition. They have learned the art of living well in spite of their limitations. Those of us coming behind, with fresh wounds and new limps, would do well to learn from the grace they give themselves and others. Sarah did that well with every person brave enough to enter her hospital room. In the midst of devastating loss, she led the way. She gave us permission to cry, cuss, laugh, sing, worship, and sit silently in the pain.

The Other Side of the Door

My friend Debbie lost her husband to a sudden heart attack several years ago. She is a huge music lover and became a friend of mine after showing up to enough of our concerts with cupcakes— a sure way to my heart. Debbie and Steve were supposed to be celebrating their anniversary, in part, by attending one of our shows, which ended up being six short weeks after he passed away. Now she would be facing the day without him. Her good friend Cate sent me an email to let me know that Debbie still wanted to come to the show and asked how I would feel about having dinner with them beforehand to honor Debbie's marriage on that first anniversary. Cate said she would be coming too and wanted to make the night as special as possible.

Good friends don't let you spend "the first" by yourself. They show up on the first birthday, Christmas, day of school, or anniversary and sit with you in the tears and sadness, the memories and longing. They show up with whatever they have, big or small, but they never let you spend the day alone. Even if you insist it's what you want. This is healing love at its best.

The week before my daughter started first grade, she picked out her best dress, fixed her hair, put on Lisa Frank press-on nails, and anxiously crossed her fingers as we drove to school to find out which teacher and classmates she would have for the upcoming year. She'd spent the entire summer praying for a certain teacher and backup teacher and hoping she would have friends from kindergarten in her new class.

When we got to the school and saw the list, I'm not sure who was more crushed—her or me. She walked quietly back to the car, without emotion, and only began to sob once we were completely off school property. When we got home she ran upstairs, slammed her bedroom door, fell to the ground, and cried for hours. I tried to go in and hold her, but she insisted on having alone time. So I gave it to her. Kind of. I sat on the other side of her door and cried with her. And then I snuck two fingers under the threshold so she would know I was there if she needed me.

An hour into the ordeal, she finally crawled over to the door and grabbed my two fingers. And there we sat, on opposite sides of the barrier between us, holding each other's fingers.

Sometimes the best thing we can do for someone in pain is sit on the other side of the door and slide our fingers under the threshold so they know they aren't alone.

Blueprint

Six weeks after Steve passed away, I sat across from Debbie and Cate at the Lemon Drop diner. We laughed, cried, and listened as she gushed on and on about her husband. Though we weren't letting her do this day alone, we also weren't sure what to expect or what to say. But Debbie showed us the way.

At one point our waitress came by and Debbie said with her typical spunk, "My husband just died and I'm ordering as many onion rings as I want!" We fell over laughing, and I asked the waitress if those could be on the house since they were a result of death. The waitress looked absolutely horrified and quickly walked away. Minutes later she returned with a free basket of onion rings, and we kept right on laugh-crying through our meal. I knew I had permission to joke with the waitress because Debbie had already given it to us through her willingness to laugh in the midst of such sorrow. She set the pace, invited us into her grief, and gave us the blueprint for walking alongside her. Allowing those who are walking through great grief to teach us how to love them well is a gift we must learn to embrace. They are our best teachers.

Only Temporary

Some people live with open wounds that fester and contaminate anyone nearby. Following them in their limpness leads to cynicism, pettiness, anger, contempt, pride, and plain ol' mean-ness. Those who have never made peace with their broken bits live tormented lives, intent on tormenting others. They feel as though everyone should have to suffer in the ways they have suffered. If they haven't, they quickly dismiss the uninjured person as spoiled and naive. They conjure up a pride that is associated with being a perpetual victim, and this becomes their boasting point. Hate grows in their heart for anyone who has it better than them; their own woundedness keeps them from living.

It's best not to model your life after a person who lives in chronic anger or despair. Their suffering has not made them empathetic toward others or attuned to the healing beauty that can be found in suffering and sorrow. Their limps have simply made them more limpy, and there is no life to be found in that. But someone who has found a way to make peace with their situation and keeps pressing into living? They are worth their weight in gold.

I was recently in Chicago O'Hare Airport, caught in the frenzy of Monday morning business travelers, when I saw an old woman who captured my heart. She was slightly hunched over and had to be in her nineties. The fact that she was purposefully walking through O'Hare Airport alone made the woman an inspiration to me. Airports are complicated these days and not laid out with the elderly in mind. Plus you have to be tough as nails to get through the Monday morning business-traveler crowd—they are vicious in their airport ninja skills and will plow you over if you get in their way. They are a lot like some hard-core cyclists. Those people aren't kidding around—they fling their arm to indicate they are turning right, and it doesn't matter if your car is headed that way or not, they aren't stopping for you.

People rushed by the old woman in the airport. Everyone going somewhere in a hurry. But not her. She stood behind her walker and slowly, step by painfully slow step, walked toward her gate. As I got closer, I noticed a piece of cardboard tied to the front of her walker with yarn. In thinly scrawled letters it read, "Only Temporary."

She didn't need my pity. But she also didn't want my oversight. She wrote the words on that poster for herself, but in so doing she invited us into her limitations and gave us a vocabulary to use as we approached her. She was not in bondage to that walker, or her body for that matter—she was free. And because of that, we could be free around her too. Her slow steps behind that walker were only temporary. I am grateful for what she taught me that day. Her acknowledgment that she was not bound by her limitations gave me permission to look my own limps in the eye and say the same thing: only temporary.

10

In the Closet

*T*here is a type of healing that waits to take us by surprise and only comes from God Himself. It cannot be planned, pursued, or purchased. A doctor cannot deliver it. No nurse, pill, exercise, therapy ball, or chiropractor can induce it. It is a gift of divine proportions.

Some healing happens at the hands of the Holy Spirit, who intercedes and works on our behalf without our asking or knowledge. When it arrives on our doorstep, it is without a shadow of a doubt a miracle. A manifestation of the Divine making Himself known. It is heaven meeting earth with an unforeseen kiss. Far removed from our efforts, it has everything to do with God's promise to redeem and restore. I call these moments Holy Spirit healings. They have happened more times than I can recall in my life. The most spectacular of which began in my closet one night.

Several years ago my little sister texted the entire family to say that one of her husband's good friends from seminary had just been violently murdered at the small church he pastored in Arlington, Texas. "Please pray," she insisted.

As the day progressed and more details came to light, I could not shake the horrible tragedy from my thoughts. It was all over the local Dallas news, and Facebook was flooded with grieved posts as friends found out about the senseless tragedy. The story was gripping: a young man had approached the front door of the church, and the senior citizen serving as secretary buzzed him in. He assaulted her, leaving her for dead, and then moved on to take the pastor's life before stealing all the money he could find and leaving. The criminal was found hours later making purchases at the mall with the pastor's credit cards; the secretary lay in a coma; and the church family began to make unexpected funeral preparations. My heart ached for the pastor's wife, his parents and siblings, and an entire church body who would soon have to walk back into the building where their young pastor had been brutally murdered and worship God.

I put my daughter to bed and went to my room to pray. The events of the day hit close to home. Though I did not know the young man who lost his life, so many people I cared for did, and they were hurting. Unable to sleep that night, I went to my closet because it was the only place in our small apartment where I could talk out loud without waking anyone up. An overwhelming sense that I needed to pray for the family had been placed deep inside me. I can count on one hand how many times I have felt such an intense, clear call to intercede on behalf of someone else the way I did that night.

At a certain point as I prayed, I sensed the Holy Spirit laying something on my heart, but I was absolutely mortified by the notion of it. My response was, "Absolutely not." I ignored the prompting and kept praying that God would send comforters to the family. But the notion came back again and again. And this is how you know God is speaking—if against all sanity and logic, the voice remains resolute and clear. Each time the voice came I politely pushed it aside. Because what kind of person finds herself in her closet at 2:00 a.m., praying for a family she does not know, when she senses the Holy Spirit telling her to track down a staff member from the church and volunteer to sing in that church three days after their pastor has been murdered? Who. Does. This?

No. I will not go to the church's website, find the email address of the worship pastor, and write a letter that says, "Dear Worship Pastor: Hello. You don't know me, but my name is Jenny and I am in a band called Addison Road and I have been praying for your church all day and the Holy Spirit told me to write you and offer to sing on Sunday morning if you are unable to lead." Nope. I absolutely will not be that crazy.

But the Holy Spirit nudge did not go away, and the longer I ignored it, the more unsettled I felt. And by unsettled I mean I felt physically unwell. I wrestled with the nudge all night, unwilling to act on it, until I finally realized it was not going away anytime soon. Sometime in the wee hours of the morning I gave in.

I googled the church, found the worship pastor's email, and shot off the most ridiculous email I have ever sent in my life. When Ryan woke up that morning, I told him what I had done, and he looked at me shocked and disturbed. "You did what? Jenny, why in the world would you do that? You can't volunteer to sing at a worship service after someone has been murdered. All the TV crews and media will be there. What if people think you are trying to steal the spotlight? You don't even know these people. Why did you do that?"

He was totally right, of course. I didn't know the family or church, and my actions could be construed through all kinds of negative filters. Logically, what I had done made no sense. I spent the better half of the morning second-guessing whether the Holy Spirit had actually told me anything in the first place and chastising myself for acting so irrationally.

The worship pastor wrote back around lunchtime.

Hi, Jenny. Clint liked your music. He saw you perform at American Airlines Arena. What if you come sing your song "Hope Now" over our congregation, and then you can be on standby if I can't get through the rest of the set? Thank you for reaching out. This will mean a lot to our congregation.

I showed up on Sunday morning still unsure of my being there. Ryan's voice—the voice of logic, social norms, boundaries, and sanity—rang in my ears. His words stung because I believed them long before he spoke them. This is how it often feels for me to follow God's voice. Jesus said He would leave us the Holy Spirit, and because of that we would be enabled to accomplish the very same things Jesus did on earth, and more. But I am slow to believe, quick to doubt, and eager to accuse myself of false motives.

Most of the time following Jesus feels like I've lost my mind. Though I usually walk out what I've been prompted to do in faith, that movement is overshadowed by a genuine sense that I have somehow made it all up and I am probably crazy. I wonder if I will ever be a part of God's work without questioning if I made it all up. One thing is certain, I will never take it lightly or boast about the tiny parts I have been given to play. Any moment that I suspect is holy ordered is a moment worth guarding and protecting, because it is either divine or I've lost my mind. Both require reverence for the serious matters at hand.

The service started and the room was filled to capacity. When it was my turn, I stepped quietly on stage and sang these words over a weeping widow, family members, and a hurting congregation: "Everything rides on hope now, everything rides on faith somehow."

When the service was over, we were the first to slip out of the building and disappear into the beautiful, sunny day. I had no idea what my purpose in being there was, or if there was a purpose. Grieved for the family, I left that morning wondering how God shows up for people like that. It wasn't until after the funeral, several weeks later, that I found out.

The Letter

Jenny,

My name is Chris, and Clint Dobson was my younger brother. You may have already heard some or all of what I write here in roundabout ways, or someone else in my family may have already written you. Please pardon me if I am repeating things you have already heard, but what I want to tell you about was one of the most significant events in my spiritual life. And you played a starring role.

The story requires background. In 2009 my sister was pregnant with her first child. She was experiencing a high-risk pregnancy, and there was concern as to whether she would be able to carry the baby full-term. It was a source of great anxiety for all of us, but Sarah and our mother carried the greatest burden.

My mom was familiar with your music because she listens to KSBJ radio and because you guys have performed at her church before. Mom loved "Hope Now" and thought it would be inspirational and helpful to Sarah as she fretted over the pregnancy.

· She bought Sarah the CD, and Sarah listened to the song every day. She carried full-term and gave birth to a beautiful and perfect daughter.

Over the next year or so Sarah did not really listen to "Hope Now." As you know, terrible things happened on Thursday, March 3, and my brother was taken from us. Two nights later as we prepared mentally to attend Sunday services at North-Pointe (a difficult prospect for us), Sarah went for a run. She took her iPod and looped "Hope Now," listening to it over and over again.

Of course, you know what happened Sunday morning at church. When you guys came so humbly, without our knowing anything about it, and sang "Hope Now," a song that has meant so much to our family, God was using you in a way you could not have known. Through you he was directly and dramatically reaching out to comfort us. The "Hope Now" event, coupled with two other important events leading up to and immediately following Clint's death, has taken what could have been a faith-shaking event and made it the most faith-inspiring series of events I have ever experienced. I wanted you to know what an important role you played in an incredible event that both comforted our family and in some very important ways strengthened my faith. God worked through you in a really big way on that Sunday. We are forever grateful to you for your part in that.

> *Sincerely,*
> *Chris*

I immediately wrote Chris back and told him about being in my closet at 2:00 a.m. and feeling like God had prompted me to reach out. About second-guessing myself and wondering if maybe I had made it up. I wanted him to know that my arriving at their church that morning was no accident. It was absolutely a divine intervention. An overwhelming prompting in my heart that I nearly refused for fear that I had absolutely lost my ever-loving mind.

Chris shared my words with their family, and his sister reached out to tell me her part of the story. This is her letter:

Jenny,

There are no words to describe the way I felt in those initial hours after learning of Clint's death. I told a minister from our church that my brain felt like it was on fire. I believe I was in shock. I decided that I had to get out of the house . . . go for a run . . . breathe in the fresh air and be able to look up to the heavens. I put on my iPod and started listening to "Hope Now" over and over again while I ran. I cried out to God about the beloved soul we had lost. I asked why and I prayed for comfort. I also prayed that God would turn this horrible event into something where He would be glorified.

As I listened to the words, "Everything rides on hope now," they couldn't have been more perfect. That is all we had in that moment . . . hope and faith.

At the end of my run, I felt some peace and comfort that I didn't have before. I felt God's presence. So when you came to NorthPointe on Sunday to sing, and you began singing "Hope Now," I truly felt that God was speaking to us through the song. He was letting us know that He was there and that He was comforting us in our time of deepest despair.

I was so amazed to read your story about feeling that God was telling you to come to NorthPointe and sing. I am so glad you shared your story. Thanks for all you have done for our family, even though you did not realize the impact of your actions at the time. God truly has used you, and is using you, for His glory and to comfort our family as we cope with the loss of Clint.

The Healer is ever at work. Even in the most painful moments when we see no glimpses of God's presence in the evil commiserating to steal, kill, and destroy around us, even then He is behind the scenes rescuing and redeeming. The truth is, we can go to the ends of the earth to seek healing, but some healing can't be found through a hospital, medicine, a support group, or a therapist. So much of our healing happens when we come face-to-face with a God who shows up in closets, on long runs after the worst news of our lives, and in sanctuaries on our hardest days. Some healing is unexplainable. It's an act of the Holy Spirit on our behalf. It helps to remember these moments and retell the stories with awe and reverence and wonder, lest we lose our ability to see miracles.

11

Emmanuel

I was once made well by a little girl in a Sunday school classroom in Texas. Thirty minutes before she healed me, I had fallen off the stage.

Fallen.

It started after I finished singing the special music during the church's main Sunday morning service. I wore heels. I never wear heels for good reason—I trip. I was certain this time would be different. But of course it wasn't.

As the song finished, I placed my mic in the holder and began to walk toward the edge of the stage. It all happened so fast. I tripped once, then put my arms out to balance myself, but it was too late. Somehow I tripped over both my feet before falling to my knees and sliding down six steep steps until I landed on the floor, five feet from the pastor, whose mouth was gaping and whose eyes looked as though he had seen a stripper walk through the doors. His face conveyed that he shared my complete humiliation. *His* humiliation may have stemmed from the fact that by the time I arrived in front of him, my knees had pulled my dress underneath me with such intensity that the spaghetti strap snapped, and beneath the sheer cardigan I was wearing, my dress had ripped, and my bra was exposed.

One thousand silent people stared at me, aghast. The pastor didn't move, neither did my bandmates on stage. No one knew what to do, and I got the distinct feeling it was my job to find a way to put everyone out of their anguished misery. Still on the floor, dress ripped, rug-burned knees, and bra exposed, I raised both hands in the air and said dramatically, "It's okay! I'm alive!" and the crowd let out an audible sigh and began to laugh uncontrollably.

I got up, confident smile on my face, shaking my head as if to say, "That silly girl!" and walked toward the back of the room as the pastor made his way on stage. He suggested a pre-sermon prayer to recenter everyone.

I quietly slipped out the back door, walked as calmly as I could until everyone was out of sight, then ducked into a dark Sunday school classroom and began to sob. I had never been so embarrassed in my entire life. Tears came fierce and childlike, barreling out of me. The sting of what happened wasn't going anywhere anytime soon, so I let it all spill out. It may well have been ten years' worth of bottled-up tears.

A little girl no more than seven years old passed by in the hallway. She heard me crying and turned around to see where the tears were coming from. Spotting me in the dark room, she stared at me for a brief moment and then disappeared. As she walked away I felt bad for her. Little innocent souls shouldn't have to see big weepy adults fall apart like that. I wished she had not seen me. Not for my own sake, but hers. She would probably talk about this moment in therapy one day, and I didn't want to add anything to her therapy list. Children have enough these days.

Her presence had startled me out of my most severe crying, though, and after she walked away I realized I had snot spiraling out of me in all sorts of unseemly ways. It was dripping down my chin and had collected in a small puddle on the table below me. My eyes were puffy and tears kept involuntarily sliding down my cheeks. As I examined the puddles of snot, I heard a small voice.

"Excuse me," she said quietly, with the most tender concern. "I brought you these."

It was the little girl. She walked into the dark room, pushed her two little fists forward, and handed me a wad of Kleenex.

She looked at me quietly for a moment, as if she had come face-to-face with an injured bunny rabbit. "Whatever it is, it's going to be better," she said quietly, then reached her hand out and patted my shoulder like she was burping a rag doll.

I nodded, knowing she was right, and smiled sheepishly. "Thank you for the Kleenex. I was very embarrassed today and that's why I'm crying. But you were brave to be so kind to me. I hope you will always be brave and kind."

Nodding, she smiled a shy, closed-mouth smile and disappeared out of the room.

In that moment she healed me. Because in that moment, she was a lot like the brave and kind Jesus. The man who steps into awkward, uncomfortable, broken spaces and brings with Him a healing balm that carries no derision. Jesus always steps into the dark Sunday school room and brings light. He is not afraid of shame or embarrassment, disease or death. Our tears and brokenness do not intimidate Him—the brokenness that we choose or the kind thrust upon us by a banged-up world. He walks right into the middle of it all, every single time, and reminds us it's going to get better.

That's My Jesus

There are no hospitals, surgeons, modern medicines, protective gloves, or surgical gowns when Jesus walks straight into a Middle Eastern slum and holds the oozing, sore-covered hands of a leper who has been abandoned by his own family and left to live in a trash heap on the unclean side of town. That's my Jesus.

When the most hated man in town shows up and climbs a tree to catch a glimpse of the radical prophet everyone is talking about, Jesus spots him and holds the man's stare. Then He announces for all to hear that He will spend the afternoon in *this* man's home. The one who collects taxes for the government of Rome. The one who inflates those numbers and pads his own pocketbook with the excesses. The one who lords power over the powerless and lies for a living. Jesus will go *there* and eat with *him*. That's my Jesus.

He lets the beautiful woman with long, flowing hair, whose past is marked by seduction, push through a room of comfortably seated men and break open her most expensive possession, pour it over His feet, and wash His dirty toes with her precious perfume. In the process, He honors her worship by protecting her heart. In that moment when all the power is His, He does not use her past against her or allow her to feel shamed, less than, or awkward. As she falls to her knees in the most vulnerable position of worship out of her deep love for Him, Jesus honors this moment by the very fact that He does not cut it short or allow His own discomfort to create a sense of shame or awkwardness. That's my Jesus.

Among the Jewish people, there were none hated as much as those who lived in Samaria. They were half-breeds, the biracial babies of pagan Assyrians and conquered Israelites. If you were traveling from the town of Galilee to the town of Jerusalem, the most direct route would take you straight through Samaria. But the pious Pharisees, who held a holy hate for Samaritans, would not be caught dead doing this. They would walk an extra half day just to avoid coming in contact with a Samaritan. Not Jesus. He headed straight into town and went to Sychar's well, where He famously asked the Samaritan woman for a drink of water and told her all He knew about her. That she had had five husbands, and the man she was currently with, her sixth, was not her husband. Then, without being asked, Jesus made His divinity known to her and told her about the secret salvation of living water He came to give. That's my Jesus.

People have sought living water since the beginning of time. Water that might save the soul. Augustus, Socrates, Plato, Aristotle, Pythagoras, rabbis, priests, prophets—Jesus could have disclosed His divinity to any number of learned and important people who were following in the footsteps of these historical thought-leaders. But He doesn't. There are only a handful of times we know of that Jesus specifically speaks about His identity. He doesn't divulge this secret to the Pharisees, Roman scholars, or famous artists of the day but instead gives His divine identity away to a low-income, biracial, sexually promiscuous woman living in a pagan town that no self-respecting Jew would ever travel through. Sharing secrets with the lowly. That's my Jesus.

He never shies away from the dark, black night. Those people we don't know what to do with? Our own moments of shame and embarrassment after we have publicly fallen? Jesus is not afraid to enter into our most broken moments. He is no avoider of pain. He walks straight up to us in the dark Sunday school room, looks deep into our eyes, and hands us a wad of Kleenex. The very essence of God's light has the power to strip away the pain, shame, and fear we may find ourselves entangled in. He is not put off or scared away by our sin or suffering. He knows well how to sit within the tension of our failures and fractures. You cannot offend His eyes—He has seen it all. And still He draws near. That's my Jesus.

In the Tension

One woman comes to mind when I think about the hours before Maggie and Ellen passed away. She met me at my sister's house to pick up my niece Abigail and to give me the burial gowns she had hand-stitched for my other nieces.

The week before, Sarah decided to have simple burial gowns made from the fabric of her wedding dress. This dear woman from the church came to pick up Sarah's wedding gown, but in the end, couldn't bring herself to use it. Instead, she cut the pattern from her *own* wedding dress. She handed me the white box and said through tears, "You don't think she is really going to need these, do you? Couldn't there still be a miracle?" We hugged and cried, not knowing what to pray for. She gave me courage to live in the tension. Because in one breath she cut up her own wedding dress and made burial gowns, and in the other she still believed for a miracle. I think Jesus honors that.

My sister Sarah wrote this about living in the tension of it all:

God sat with me today at Maggie and Ellen's grave as I cried and spoke of my hurt. He sat quietly and allowed me to explore and express my feelings and pain, the true and untrue, rational and irrational. God welcomed me and my feelings with grace, peace, understanding, and kindness. I wasn't met with frustration or hostility, anger or unrealistic expectations. The bearer of all burdens gently took nine weeks' worth of hurt and held that pain with me. I serve a God who isn't afraid to enter into the mess of our world. That is mercy.

Eventually I got up, wiped my eyes, and walked away from the grave, feeling empty but alive, hurt but not alone. That is a miracle. I've relearned that God is gracious, slow to be frustrated by my questions, and abounding in steadfast love. God never hurries me down the road of grief. God knows this road well and isn't intimidated by it. God is and always will be with us. Emmanuel.

One of the best sermons I've heard in my life was about the tension of living in between Emmanuel and Epiphany. "We long for Epiphany," the pastor said, "but the beauty of the story is not Epiphany. The beauty is Emmanuel." The angel Gabriel showed up and revealed the plans to Mary, the star showed up to guide those who would follow its light, and the hosts of angels appeared to the shepherds the night Jesus was born. But then they all disappeared. The angel, the star, and the choir of heavenly hosts. Gone. Even Jesus, the pastor said, appeared in the room of disciples, allowing Thomas to stick his fingers into the wounded flesh. And then? Just as quickly as He miraculously appeared—He disappeared. Epiphanies come and go. Emmanuel is constant.[1]

As we drove to church to celebrate Epiphany this year, Annie announced that when the time came to reenact the journey, she was going to be a shepherd—not an angel. We knew ahead of time that all the kids would be given materials to create their own costumes and encouraged to be a shepherd, wise man, or angel. After the costumes were hastily assembled, the lights would be turned off and the room illuminated by Christmas lights surrounding a manger scene. The story of the shepherds and wise men following the angels and star to find baby Jesus would be read aloud while Christmas carols played in the background. And after it was all over, there would be a king's cake for the children to devour.

I asked Annie why she wanted to be a shepherd, and she said, "Well, I really want to be the star that dances through the sky and leads people to Jesus, but if I can't be the star, I just want to be lying in a field of grass when it comes out of nowhere to light up everything. Can you imagine, Mom?!"

I told her I couldn't imagine, and that it would have been even more surprising and exciting back then, because people couldn't just go to a computer and google "big, bright, shiny star shows up out of nowhere" and figure out where the star came from and why.

"Yeah," she said, "I guess the angels were kind of like Google telling the shepherds why the star came." She got quiet and blew hot air onto the cold car window and drew a picture of herself. "Mom, why doesn't God send us a big, bright star anymore and show us where Jesus is? I would follow it."

My heart sighed. Oh, how I long for a bright star leading me to the exact place where Jesus is, illuminating exactly what comes next on the journey. I would follow it too. It is human nature to want to see God manifested right before our eyes, to see a brilliant star set ablaze for the sole purpose of leading us straight to Jesus—but that's not what we always get.

What we get is the unseen.

What we get is Emmanuel.

And Emmanuel never came in the ways we were looking for in the first place.

12

Soul Nurses

I come from a long line of nursing. When I was young, my dad's mom worked behind the front desk of a small clinic in Enterprise, Mississippi. Although she was not technically a nurse, that didn't stop her from administering one too many suppositories over the course of my vomit-laden childhood. I threw up *all* the time as a little girl. Before birthdays, Christmas, Easter, family vacations, or any other life moment that caused me to become "too excited." The problem was, once I started throwing up I couldn't stop. I would often throw up until all that was coming out were the last little bits of green bile lining my stomach.

Two decades later a counselor would finally say, "You do know that is called *anxiety*, right? And anxiety that leads to a childhood of vomiting is a pretty serious form of anxiety?"

Well, no, lady. We *didn't* know that. I was just an "excited" child. And so I spent the better half of my early childhood getting suppositories up the booty from my Mamaw, who got them at the clinic where she wasn't a nurse but might as well have been. She called them magic bullets, and I am here to tell you they were *not* magical at all. Anytime I started throwing up, I knew what was coming for me out of the refrigerator, icy cold.

Mamaw's daughter would go on to become a nurse and then a nurse practitioner. My earliest memories of Aunt Terri's nursing skills are from Mamaw and Papaw's bedroom where my dad, his brother, and all the boy cousins would line up to receive their weekly allergy injections. I wanted no part of this. I would rather sneeze to death than go to that bedroom and get in the shot line.

Later, we would bring to her every ailment, injury, and mental breakdown in hopes she could diagnose and cure us. I think she can cure anything. Whether she likes it or not, she has become the in-house healer for our family. I still text her a list of symptoms when my own daughter is sick and pepper her with questions until I am convinced she isn't hiding anything from me and it really probably is *just* a cold.

My dad, thank goodness, is not a nurse. His bedside dad jokes might make you want to jump out of the hospital window. He did, however, become the on-site chaplain for a major nursing school in Dallas when I was in junior high. On days when my sisters and I would visit him at the office, we would always be asked by an eager fourth-year nursing student if we wanted to be practiced on. "Practice what?" we would fearfully ask. "Drawing blood!" was always the answer. No. Thank. You. I realize nurses have to practice drawing blood, inserting PICC lines, and doing Pap smears on someone, but I am *not* that someone.

When I was a junior in high school, my dad brought me on one of the medical mission trips that the soon-to-be nurses took to the Texas/Mexico border. These juniors and seniors in college weren't spending their spring break in Panama City Beach binge drinking; they were spending it in Mexico bandaging wounds.

I was amazed when a little boy around six years old waited for nearly an entire day to be seen, and when his turn finally came, his parents explained that he could not hear well anymore. He hadn't been born with hearing issues, but for over a year he had suffered what appeared to be major, unexplained hearing loss. The boy looked terrified. All these nice, young, pretty girls in lab coats with stethoscopes were a sight unseen for him—he had never been seen by a doctor in his life. The girls spoke broken Spanish to him, offered him a teddy bear, and made him smile and giggle. And then they peered into his ears and found rocks.

The little boy, or perhaps a sibling, had put two tiny rocks in his ears. They did not come out easily, but one hour later, with many tears and a crowd of onlookers, he could hear again. It was the first time I remember thinking that some of the world's greatest miracles happen because nurses and doctors show up and do their jobs well. The Holy Spirit seemed to confirm the thought in my heart and mind: *Yes, I perform miracles through the very hands of those who show up and offer their hands to be used.* It was a profound moment in my faith life in which I seriously contemplated becoming a nurse in order to be a part of miracle making.

But on the drive home from El Paso to Dallas in that cramped sixteen-passenger van, the *almost* nurses chatted incessantly about bowel movements, chest compressions, and catheter bags, and I started feeling queasy. No, I did not want to tell them how many times I had pooped since we had been away from home. My nursing dreams ended there.

The older you get, the more grateful you become for nurses. The kind who draw blood and give your children shots while magically distracting them. The kind who teach you how to do a breast exam or prepare you for a prostate exam. The kind who change colostomy bags, coach mommas through one more big push, and make sure the morphine drip keeps those we love comfortable until heaven and earth collide. The kind who work well beyond their shifts to help your sister give birth and cry right along with the family when the babies don't live. The kind of nurse who writes your sister a card afterward to say, "Thank you for letting me be there with you—it was an honor. And just think, when they opened their eyes they saw Jesus." How could we live without nurses?

When my Grandpa was admitted to the hospital, we knew he was sick but didn't assume it would be his last night to speak. Not being in the same state as him was hard for me, but it was harder on my mom and his other daughters. As soon as I heard he was headed to the hospital, I texted my baby cousin on my dad's side of the family. (Calling him *my baby cousin* is a bit misleading, even though he *is* nine years younger than me. Chris is six feet two and built like a linebacker, with the heart of a teddy bear. I am always trying to get him married off to someone who is worthy of him, though no girl has quite measured up yet. I think with his tender heart and rugged Mississippi boyishness, he is pretty near perfect.) I texted Chris because he is a nurse. The kind of nurse who, though he lived thirty minutes away from my Grandma and Grandpa, would often drive over just to check on them and look at my Grandpa's legs to make sure the infection wasn't spreading and his bandages were on properly. Did I mention he might be a saint? I'm pretty convinced.

Chris works emergency room triage at the hospital my Grandpa was admitted to, and though I knew it was a long shot, I wondered if he might be working the night Grandpa was admitted. Chris quickly texted back—he was on that night and would be up to check on him as soon as he could get away from the ER. He talked to Grandpa and reassured Grandma before she left for the night. Four a.m. was the last time he went in to check on him; he was complaining about being cold and the lights being too bright. My cousin was the last person to hear Grandpa's voice this side of heaven. He holds a treasure.

Nurses carry the sounds of our deepest pains, our brightest joys, and our most treasured people. Theirs is hard and holy work. Many nurses take an oath before practicing their profession. The most popular is known as the Florence Nightingale Pledge. The last line of the oath states, "With loyalty will I endeavor to aid the physician in his work, and devote myself to the welfare of those committed to my care."[1]

This is a beautiful pledge for a nurse to make, and it is also a beautiful pledge for a Christian to make. In much the same way nurses in the medical community bridge the gap between patient and doctor, soul nurses bridge the gap between the hurting and the Healer. The same oath can apply to those who take seriously the call of Christ to care for the broken in body, mind, spirit, and soul. For those who loyally endeavor to aid the Great Physician in His work and devote themselves to the care of those who have been committed to them.

Heavy Lifting

Three days after the girls died, I flew back to Tennessee in a daze. My counselor and psychiatrist would later tell me that the extreme events of those days led to a shock that was consistent with post-traumatic stress disorder. Apparently sitting in a room with two little girls who aren't breathing is powerful enough to trigger a tsunami inside of you. And it did. I came home from the hospital experiencing a type of shock that I had never known and was ill-prepared to handle. Miraculously enough—I came home to nurses.

My mother- and father-in-law had bought airline tickets to come to Nashville and visit us months before during a Southwest Airlines mega fare sale. There was no real reason for them to come to Nashville that particular week, barring the fact that the tickets were cheap. I arrived home to food cooking on the stove and someone else able to take care of my daughter. My in-laws cooked and played with Annie while Ryan worked and made sure there were clean clothes to wear and groceries in the refrigerator. I stayed in bed for nearly forty-eight hours. I was in a dazed, out-of-body state the rest of the week as the funeral drew near. Looking back, I am convinced that my in-laws purchasing tickets for that specific week—months before, during a fare special—was no less than God preparing the way for me and making sure I came home to nurses.

Soul nurses are the people who show up in your hardest moments and care for you when you cannot care for yourself. They do the heavy lifting. Sometimes they are in-laws who have a trip planned at just the right moment or a cousin working the night shift. Sometimes they show up with chicken spaghetti or offer to take your kids for the night (and push you out the front door whether you are ready or not). Other times they lay in bed with you until the tears deplete your body of all that's left and you finally fall asleep. There are chapters in our stories when the pain and shock are so overwhelming that we simply cannot process the brokenness at hand and can no more care for ourselves than we can change the circumstances. It is in those moments that soul nurses grab the baton and run for us.

I love the Bible story of the paralytic man whose friends carry him across town on a mat to Jesus, the Healer. When they find that the crowds gathered have become too dense to get through, these friends do not give up. They climb to the roof and begin to dig a hole big enough to lower their paralytic friend in from the top. When one man is incapable of securing his healing, his friends faithfully see to it that he is brought straight to the Healer. This is what we are called to do for one another.

Author Robert Benson describes the moment in his own journey when he was not well enough to seek healing for himself. When Jesus offered to make him well, he says he was too sick to say yes. Instead it was his sister and his nurse, Norma, who fought for his healing when he could not do so.

> In the dark when Christ came to me as I lay here on my mat in the glare of the brake light—or was it in the dust, begging alms at the city gate, or beside the pool whose waters promised healing if only I could reach them in time, or along the road where one could make mud for the eyes from spittle and dirt, or on the road to Mary and Martha's house, where the crowd jockeyed for position and a good seat, or in the tomb with Lazarus himself, wrapped in bandages, beginning to rot, alone in the dark—on the day when Christ said to me, "Do you want to be healed?" it was Norma who kept saying yes, not me. I was too tired, too ill, too afraid, too uncertain, too ready to die. It was Norma and my sister and my friends and a couple of dozen strangers who took me to the healer.[2]

When I think back over my life, to my own dark nights of the soul, I remember my inability to care for myself and the nurses who have come to my rescue. Not the kind of nurses who put an IV into my arm but the kind who put an IV into my heart. Pushing the fluids I needed to stay alive, bringing spirit to carry me when I had none. There were nurses tending to my soul (and my house) during those very dark moments, and they kept me alive. Friends, strangers, doctors, neighbors, nurses, and ministers who are willing to do the heavy lifting and care for the most broken among us—they are the living, breathing hands and feet of God Himself.

After Barbara Brown Taylor experienced a serious head injury, she said, "The first miracle of this time was that people took care of me when I could not care for myself."[3] That we show up for one another time and time again and carry one another to the Healer is nothing short of a miracle.

Soul Nurses

I would have never thought of the idea of being a soul nurse to someone had Lacy not asked me. I met Lacy at a worship event during one of the hardest seasons of her life. Her daughter had recently told her she was being sexually assaulted by her step-father—*Lacy's husband*. This incredibly brave mom called the police, and her husband was arrested, investigated, and stood charges for multiple statutory rape counts. He was sentenced to a lengthy stay in prison. She would later learn that her other daughter had shared the same horror story. Lacy was left with all the pieces: both daughters in therapy, one income, gaping wounds, starting all over again.

She had hoped her daughters would never experience the kind of trauma and abuse that she had experienced as a little girl, and she lived with the guilt, shame, and anger of not knowing that the man she loved was preying on her own children. The weekend we met, I was able to spend precious time with her family and remind them that they were not walking alone, they were loved, and by God's strength they could take each step required of them. Their story would be one of redemption and restoration.

As we parted ways, Lacy promised to keep in touch, and I promised to encourage her in the small ways that I could. She sent this letter my way one evening:

Jenny,

The last month has not been fun. In fact, I think emotionally it's been the worst one so far out of the last several years. Just this weekend, however, I was able to come up with an analogy to see this time in my life as labor pains. They will come and go, and eventually, when they stop, new life will have been birthed from going through all of this.

I did not handle childbirth as well as some . . . I wanted the drugs to take the edge off, I swore worse than a sailor, but I did make it through. I was in active labor with both of my kids for four days before they were finally born. And as soon as I saw them, the pain, the experience, every bad thing that happened during labor, immediately went to the back of my mind and I was instead filled with love and joy. An all-encompassing love and joy.

I hope this journey is like that. I know that there will be good days (in between the contractions/labor pains) and then the really bad days. These days are not fun, but they are necessary. And I know I can't get through the delivery alone. Just like birthing a baby, it's not meant to be done alone. We need others at our sides for support so we don't give up, to remind us the end

is near, nurses to care for us . . . and the doctor there overseeing
everything in case of an emergency and for the grand finale.

I want Jesus to be my doctor in life. I know I can't do life
anymore without Him. I am trying to choose to look at these
episodes as horrid labor pains. But a labor pain does the work
necessary, and once that pain is gone, I will have a beautiful
life! And my heart will no longer be broken but will be sewn
back together by my Great Physician. Will you continue to be
one of my nurses as I am working through these labor pains? I
have only made it this far because you are by my side.

Love,
Lacy

Has there ever been a more beautiful invitation? I've received
a lot of good requests in my life, but none this profound. To be
asked to become someone's soul nurse is a heartfelt treasure. It
was one of the most moving invitations of my life. One that I
felt severely underqualified for.

Lacy,

As I read and reread your letters, what strikes me most is
not the absolute hell you are walking through but the fact that
Jesus seems to be so strongly, beautifully, wisely, graciously,
and protectively leading you through. You have every right to
be afraid, exhausted, bitter, burned-out, or even hopeless based
on the trauma and pain you have had to walk your precious
daughters through. And yet, what I read is not that. It's not those
things. I read peace that passes understanding. I read wisdom
and hope that looks far beyond these temporary birthing pains
and instead sees new life. You are absolutely right—these are

labor pains. And they are indeed brutally painful. But you are so close to turning the corner. So close to seeing new life. And I am incredibly awed by your ability to see that new life and to place your HOPE in it. God WILL BIRTH NEW LIFE from the ruins. He always does.

I am praying Psalm 139 over you this morning and every time I think of you. That your eyes, ears, and heart would be wide open to the fact that God goes before you, behind you, and all around you and hems you in. That you would feel hemmed in by the very Spirit of God, who protects what this world tries to break. He protects his daughters. He hems us in. I pray that you and the girls would overwhelmingly sense that.

I feel like I have such a small, tiny part in your story and journey toward new life, but I am forever grateful for it. I love your invitation to be a nurse. I accept, though you should know I suck at blood and pain. Maybe I am a better doula. Or the creepy night nurse who only comes in to change the colostomy bag. Just saying.

Much Love,
Jenny the night nurse

13

Kisses and Confession

My daughter, Annie, is sensitive in every sense of the word. Sensitive to the feelings of others and to her own feelings and to our cats' feelings. Sensitive to the textures of food, the feel of her socks, and the hems on every outfit. In my lesser moments of motherhood, I have threatened to saw her feet off if we have to try on *one more pair* of socks. "I will render you footless," I have barked in frustration. She is sensitive to lyrics in songs, scenes on TV, and the lives of characters found in the pages of children's books we read.

Once we were in a remote island area in the country of Belize, sitting on a giant patio couch overlooking the most picturesque ocean I have ever seen in my life, when the song "Paradise" by Coldplay came on. As the chorus rolled over me like a wave, I dug my toes in the sand and pinched myself. It was one of the most surreal moments of my entire life—it *was* paradise. Annie, on the other hand, leaned over and whispered, "Mom, this is the saddest song I've ever heard." While I was focusing on the single word *paradise*, she was focusing on the verses, which are about a little girl praying to escape her broken reality, praying to wake up in paradise. The song wrecked my daughter's heart, and to this day she will ask me to change the radio station if it happens to come on. Annie's sensitivity astounds me.

When she was five years old she overheard Ryan and me talking about going to the church to get it set up for the home-less community who would be spending the night there that evening. Temperatures in Nashville were dangerously low, and churches around the city were opening their doors to offer the homeless community a warm place to spend the night. As we drove home from church, I told Ryan I was going to call some neighbors and see if anyone had extra pillows and blankets for me to collect, then I would head back up to the church and help get it ready for the incoming guests.

Annie took all this in from the backseat and said, "I want to go!"

Ryan looked at me hesitantly; he was worried she might be in the way.

"I don't know, baby," I told her nonchalantly. "I'm not sure if today is a good day for that." (Insert: Worst mom answer ever. Today is not a good day for my child to voluntarily come to church and help get it set up for homeless people? Really?!)

"Mom," she said matter-of-factly, "I am going to the church with you and I am bringing stuffed animals. If the homeless people are spending the night in a new place where they've never been before, during a storm, they are going to need stuffed animals to snuggle with." And that was that.

139

I thought by the time we finished lunch and got home, she would forget her altruistic notions and go play. But she didn't. She went straight to her bedroom and started sorting through her stuffed animals and picking out the ones she wanted to bring. A short time later she asked me how to spell the word *snuggling*, and one hour later she emerged with a sign decorated in stickers reading, "For Snuggling. Love Annie." When I explained to her that she might not get her stuffed animals back or that they might get dirty, she said she didn't care and reiterated that it was going to be dark and the homeless people would be in a new place and probably a little bit scared, and they would definitely need animals to snuggle with.

That afternoon she taught me what love looks like.

As Annie's mom, I am both awed and terrified by her sensitivity. Awed because she has much to teach the world about empathy, compassion, grace, and real love. Terrified because she bruises easily. What bounces right off one child's chest sticks to Annie's heart. She internalizes everything and forgets nothing.

When I began piecing Annie's personality and character traits together, I realized that her heart must be weighed down with all that she was internalizing and carrying around, and I needed to find a way to lighten her load. So one night I told her that God loves to take away fear, worry, sadness, or anything else heavy that we might be holding on to inside of us. If we give those things to God, I told her, He would keep them and send us His peace and love to take their place.

She thought about it for a minute and asked, "How do we get it to Him? The bad things?"

I love this thoughtful response. She's pragmatic, and I wanted her to physically experience handing over these things, so without much thought I said, "Well, we throw them up to God. And

He catches them. So if you have anything in your heart that you want to get rid of, we can just try to see if it works."

She spent the next thirty minutes detailing *all the things* weighing her down. My heart broke for her.

Not a word was spoken in our home, at school, with her friends, or on the radio that she hadn't heard and internalized. We put our hands close to her heart, and I said a little prayer. "God, Annie belongs to You and not to these emotions or fears. She is ready to give these things to You, and we ask that You take them far away and replace them with Your love and peace." Then we scooped out all the worry, embarrassment, and fear, and with full hands and clinched fists we hurled them toward the ceiling of her bedroom.

As our hands made their way back down, Annie's hand landed on my forehead. "Look, Mom, God sent us down kisses!" Her tiny fingers touched my forehead and slid down to my nose, then dragged over to my left cheek and then my right, as if she were making the sign of the cross right there on my face with the kisses of Christ.

There I was trying to give my daughter an outlet for her worry, and she was giving me the gifts of healing. Tears fell from my eyes as I experienced the kind of love that takes up our worry and sends back kisses. It never occurred to me that she might tangibly experience a transaction with heaven, but she did. God always sends something to fill the place where the wound is. Through our confession, we were being made well.

On Confession

I grew up in a faith background that did not put much emphasis on corporate confession. We did not confess to a priest on

Sunday, and while we were certainly instructed to share our sins with God, there were hardly any times I can remember where I was encouraged to confess to another person. By the time I got to college, "accountability partners" were all the rage and everyone was confessing, but it felt more like self-flagellation and a merit-based system than anything else. It didn't aim at healing and moving forward as much as it did carrying on about how awful we were as humans and how little we had earned or deserved. Often the confessions weren't kept safe and were used against you in a way that brought about waves of guilt and shame. And sometimes the confessions managed to make their way to the larger group—so everyone would know "how to pray for you."

I left those circles as quickly as possible, but I also left behind the gift of communal confession. "Confession is a means of grace," author James Bryan Smith says. "It is a privilege, not a duty. Confession is an activity whereby we invite God to begin working on what has been destroying us. It is not so much an attempt to rid ourselves of the past as it is a way by which we live in union with God."[1]

For over a decade, confession in my life looked like the Jesus prayer—"Lord Jesus Christ, Son of God, have mercy on me, a sinner"—followed by my own personal, private time of divulgence. It wasn't until very recently, in my midthirties, that I found myself in the active rhythms of weekly, communal confession. I was invited by a close friend to join her and two other moms for a weekly time of sharing our sins. Immediately I cringed. Nothing sounded worse than four women sitting around talking about how terrible we were. She assured me that this was a safe group and the point of our time together would be life giving even in the midst of speaking our darkest and dirtiest sins out loud. I had my doubts.

At our first gathering we sat outside a coffee shop, and my friend, the one who organized the group, told us how this would all work. The one confessing was the only one able to speak. No one else could empathize, agree, share their own story, or add any input. The temptation to dampen a confessor's confession was too strong. For instance, I might say, "I was horrible to my husband this week. I mean, I think he started it, but I certainly didn't let it end there, because how *hard is it* to pay me a compliment?" And then the other girls might jump in with, "I hear your confession, but seriously, you are smoking hot and he *should* be dishing out the compliments! My husband should be too, for that matter." And before you know it we are not confessing; we are blaming and cajoling one another in our gripes against humanity. This is not true confession, which is aimed at repentance. This is gossipy girl talk. There is a big difference.

Empathy, shortcuts, and a lessening of one another's guilt, my friend said, were not the appropriate responses to someone else's confession. We could only listen. Also, after you confessed you were to express a goal about how you hoped to work on this area of your life or how you envisioned a different way of moving forward. We would all share and then we would pray.

My friend went first. Once she finished, another girl in the group surprised us all by reaching across the table and grabbing her hand. She looked her square in the eyes and said, "I hear your confession of being an angry mother and not using your time wisely. I hear your desire to create peace in your home this next week and treat the members of your family with more patience and kindness. You are forgiven by God. And you are loved by God and by us."

Tears welled up in my friend's eyes. Though she was the organizer of this whole confession experiment, she'd never expected those kisses from heaven to fall on her face.

The other girl quickly said, "I learned that from an older lady in our church who taught us the gift of receiving confession. I hope that's okay."

It was more than okay. It was perfect. Now I look forward to the one afternoon each week I sit on a porch somewhere and offer my confession. Because I know it will be followed by a hand reaching over to hold mine, reminding me that I am forgiven by God and loved by the other three women sitting at the table.

Sparkly Clean

The tradition Annie and I started has grown and expanded since that first night of throwing our angst up to God. First grade has proven to be an unforeseeably difficult year of school for Annie, and she insists on taking several handfuls of stress out of her chest before she is finally able to collect all her angst. Before throwing these handfuls up, we offer a confessional prayer that goes something along these lines: "God, thank You for being here with us. We are sorry for the times we hold on to the worry and stress inside of us, and we are saddened by the times it sticks to our hearts without our permission. We don't want it. We give it to You tonight and ask that You please carry it for us and send us Your peace and love instead."

After we throw our fistfuls up, Annie often takes to a spastic shaking of her hands to make sure she has gotten all the crumbs off. Then come the kisses from heaven. One night she added, "Mom, I feel like after kisses tonight, God just cleaned my heart off with His hands and made it sparkly." So now, after kisses, we rub one another's chests right above our hearts, cleaning it all off, and then Annie gives herself a big hug and hugs me. We do this every single night. And truth be told, some nights I just want to get on with it already. There are so many steps and so many confessions and so many exchanges of hugs, kisses, worry, peace, and self-hugs. We are like our own Catholic Mass. And all I really want is a glass of wine on the couch while I watch Colbert on TV.

But each night I am learning the importance for my own soul of being in Annie's room, handing things—or hurling them, in our case—over to God. Sure, I can make it four or five or fifteen days without detailing the state of my heart and confessing the broken bits inside, but when I do this, I miss those kisses falling from the sky—ointment for my wounds. There is something about the daily gift of confession and turning over the things stuck in my heart that is bringing about a more joyful spirit in me.

It is in the art of practicing daily confession that I am brought before a God who longs to daily, hourly, moment by moment, send down kisses from heaven to cover me. When I let my soul get backlogged, I never seem to get ahead. Then I get caught up in guilt. My specialty. When I finally crawl out from under the rock of shame, I have a laundry list so long that it feels like I am starting over again from square one. I am making up for lost time instead of moving forward. When I practice the art of daily confession (even if it *is* just in my daughter's bedroom at night), there are some days I realize my heart and soul are incredibly light and free.

On a recent night I asked Annie if she had anything she wanted to throw up to God. She paused and said, "I don't think so, Mom. I've got nothing. What about you?"

I thought for a long second and answered, "I actually don't think I have anything either!"

She laughed and said, "Well, I guess our lives are good!" And we both died laughing.

When confession and relinquishing control become daily habits, it becomes easier to live free. Each day we are learning to live under the grace of being sparkly clean.

Jump off the Train

$\mathcal{I}$ was traveling with my band, Addison Road, through Amsterdam when I stumbled into one of the best nights of my life. I traveled with the kind of guys who religiously followed maps and Siri's voice. If Siri said, "Turn right in five hundred feet," it did not matter that we were supposed to be going the opposite direction or that turning right meant driving directly into a mall parking lot or a dead-end street. If Siri said it, they were apt to follow it. I suppose this saved us endless hours of fighting over whose directions were right; all blame could squarely fall on the voice at the other end of our cell phones' inanimate GPS. Still, by the end of my time on the road with my map-loving husband and bandmates, I despised Siri and reckoned I knew more than she did at least half the time.

When I first began to travel, I entered cities as a girl on a mission, with carefully curated itineraries highlighting the best restaurants, museums, historic districts, and pubs. I wanted to see everything, preferably in order from my first step off the subway or out of my hotel lobby. Before tours began, I studied cities and came armed with pages of printed suggestions for what we might do while visiting Bangor or Birmingham.

But as the years went by and I visited major cities three, four, and five times, my explorer spirit began to wane. Toward the end of my time in Addison Road, I no longer desired carefully crafted excursions after long days on a bus or plane; I simply longed for rest. At that point in my extensive travel life, if I were to experience something new in a city, I wanted it to be a spontaneous discovery—the result of a girl set free to explore and get lost for a bit. And that is exactly what happened in Amsterdam.

We went to Amsterdam divided. And by divided, I mean all of the guys in the band had a game plan for our two days off in the city. They had restaurants, museums, and pubs pinpointed on the map and Siri in their back pocket, ready to give step-by-step walking directions. I had nothing but a romantic notion of getting lost on the meandering streets and sipping lattes at cafés along the city's famous canals. Ryan and I agreed that we would stick with our bandmates as far as the main train station in the heart of the city, but after that I had no intentions of trekking to the Anne Frank museum or any other predetermined points of interest. It was because of this loose grip on the day's plans that when I saw a mob of people swarming around a canal ten stops before the main station, I decided to jump off.

As we pulled up to the train stop, I could see people outside pressing forward into a commotion I could not yet see. The canals were completely jammed as well. It was impossible for a single boat to get through. No one seemed to be going anywhere, and I immediately assumed it was a riot or political movement. This was a *far* more exciting prospect than anything on the guys' agendas, and since I didn't have anywhere to be, my detective spirit got the best of me and I bolted.

Ryan was furious at my impulsiveness. In all honesty, it wasn't responsible or kind of me to just decide without any forethought or warning that I was going to exit the train ten stops early— without the rest of my group. Splitting up the group in such a huge, unknown international city wasn't great traveling-with-friends etiquette. But I had a hunch that something crazy was happening and I wanted to see what it was.

Ryan barely made it off the train with me, and we immediately found ourselves in a throng of people pressing into one another. We began to look for any indication of police presence or political protestors but saw nothing. People were pleasant and chatty, there wasn't a cloud in the sky, and the cobblestone path lining the canal was as dreamy as I had imagined. Without any real direction or idea of what was happening, we followed the ebb and flow of the crowd slowly moving us forward until we came upon what was causing the large gathering of people.

Right in the middle of the canal, a mile from the train stop, was a temporary stage surrounded by lights and small boats. I heard a man behind me speaking in English and was finally able to ask someone what was happening.

His face lit up. "Oh! You do not know?" He seemed excited to be the one inviting me into one of the city's finest secrets. "Once a year the symphony comes to this spot on the canal, builds a stage, and plays all night under the stars for free. Everyone brings their blankets, wine, cheese, and pastries and enjoys an absolutely delightful treat. You must stay; you will only get a spot if you come now! You are on perfect time!"

I love being on perfect time. Especially if a beautiful man with a dreamy European accent on a thousand-year-old cobblestone road tells me I'm *on perfect time!*

What ensued was arguably the most magical night of my entire life. I will always remember it as a "pinch me, I'm dreaming" experience. And these types of memorable experiences are crucial in our healing journeys.

These kinds of moments have a way of adding up in the heart and fortifying the lining of a life. A preemptive healing of sorts, strengthening your memory bank and arteries the way a daily dose of fish oil might. So when the hard times come, the arteries don't give way without a fight. They are lined with memories so rich and deep that healing is already living inside you like a mighty omega-3, warding off would-be blood-clotting enemies. So keep those moments with you. Store up the awe and wonder of every unexpected gift of a moment and let them line the arteries of your life as healing oils.

Write the memories down. Share the stories time and time again. Give thanks for every good gift, every twist in the story that takes you by surprise. The prophets in the Old Testament often spurred the Israelite people to "remember!" Perhaps they knew that the memory of God's faithfulness was enough to carry a person through a long, weary season of doubt and destruction. Remember those once-in-a-lifetime moments. They are more than glossy photos for Facebook; they are the fortifiers of our faith. They carry with them the power to preemptively heal.

In my experience, "pinch me, I'm dreaming" moments almost never happen when I'm actually *trying* to be on perfect time and almost always happen when I decide to jump off the train and follow a hunch. Some of life's most salvaging moments come without a script and Siri's voice telling me to turn left in five hundred feet. Sometimes you end up in Amsterdam on a blanket under the stars, with a world-renown symphony playing Beethoven and your closest friend by your side, because you are tired of plans and are no longer a person on a mission—just a person not wanting to miss the hunchy moments, a person willing to jump off the train a time or two.

If there is a chance that healing comes in unexpected ways, we have to be willing to hold on to our plans loosely and follow unexpected paths. When we do, we often stumble upon our being-made-well experiences—those moments most worth remembering.

15

Sacred Pauses

My grandparents had two acres of a front yard, guarded by a faded white plank fence, soaring pine trees, and fierce red ants. Grandma put plastic deer and American flags in the grass and worked the flower beds and tree beds with careful attention. She cultivated the yard the way some people cultivate friendships, furiously and with fervor. She may well die in her front yard with a hummingbird on her shoulder and a plastic garden animal in her hands. I can think of no better ending for her.

After weekend lunches and Sunday dinners, Grandpa always invited us to join him on his daily walk. He walked the length of the two acres just to get to the end of the street that ran alongside the house. Then he walked half that as he turned left and made the distance past the front of his vast yard and finally on to the next home where Coach lived. Coach's two dogs always followed behind. Past Coach's house there were a few other homes, though I barely remember them because they belonged to the Mississippi woods and I had my suspicions. The road in front of Grandpa's house was narrow and hardly driven, bumpy with age and attitude. On the right was a pasture with no cows, set between two rolling hills and a pond long forgotten, green and mossy. The smell of honeysuckle and hay filled the air.

Grandpa always walked this road, past the pond. But on long afternoons he made his way down the quiet concrete, past Coach's house, to the fork in the road and then took the sharp right, which meant he was prepared to walk the entire length of the pasture that surrounded the pond. My heart fluttered as he turned right. This extra part of the walk was not for the faint of heart. Coach's dogs gave up and turned back around at the fork to head home. I soared. Though my feet ached, my belly grumbled, and I rarely had anything to contribute to the conversation, I felt as privileged as any child could. Grandpa talked loudly, excitedly, and argumentatively over whatever issue needed debating—instinctively slowing down when we kids needed a minute to catch up. I walked knowing I was loved and wanted. Always invited down the road, though I had nothing to offer.

When the house sold, I thought I would crumble for want of that road and those walks, those twilight hours when I absolutely belonged. On that road I was home. Nowadays, in between my travel schedule for work, family and friends spread out across the country, and my parents living in a house and a town I did not grow up in, I often ache for home, but I'm not sure I know where that is. "But where, after we have made the great decision to leave the security of childhood and move on into the vastness of maturity, does anybody ever feel completely at home?" Madeleine L'Engle asks.[1] Maturity feels more vast than I am comfortable with.

Modern society and its endless opportunities also feel more vast than I am comfortable with. Madeleine L'Engle's words were written long before Facebook, Amazon's two-hour delivery, and iEverything. We live in an unprecedented time in history when information, goods, and social statuses change hands, feeds, and souls in record speed. It is all flying, whizzing, whirling by. Quiet roads where we belong are hard to come by. One can belong to everything and everyone, and most of us over-belong ourselves in our quest to find home. We belong to so many people and so many things that when we sit still long enough, we recognize the gnawing feeling that we aren't deeply known by anyone.

There are *all the groups*. Facebook groups and book launch groups. Community groups, Bible study groups, MOPS, civic organizations, PTA, rowing teams, running clubs, gardening groups, supper clubs, and neighborhood associations. And then there are all of the secondary groups that you are involuntarily roped into through children, spouses, and co-workers.

There are *all the charities*. Over 1.5 million registered nonprofits in the United States alone. The opportunities to give back, invest, and live missionally are everywhere. How does one even know where to begin?

Then there are *all the friends*. Facebook, Twitter, Instagram, Periscope, and other social media friends who become real-life friends. Which is a thing now. A new friend just stayed at my house on her one-day layover in Nashville. I met her through my blog and kept up with her through Facebook. She flew in from her home in New Zealand, and we sat on the porch all night under the stars, sipping wine and swapping ministry stories.

These types of friendships were not everyday realities twenty years ago, but now they are. We can sit on the back porch with someone from halfway around the world and call him or her friend. There are virtual friends and real-life friends. Friends from different circles—our childhood, work, church, neighborhood, our children's schools and colleges—and the people we accidentally meet and connect with at Starbucks or on the airplane. Is it any wonder we are overwhelmed with our schedules, overcommitted in our relationships, and confused about where we actually belong? Who of us can figure out where we belong when we give ourselves to everyone? No wonder it feels stressful—we are the most socially advanced and interconnected society history has ever known. And we are exhausted.

I recently sat down to have my hair done, and the Aveda stylist explained that she would begin by giving me an oil treatment and head massage. She had an array of oils I could choose from, but she wanted me to close my eyes while I smelled each one so I wouldn't pick based on the oil's name. I closed my eyes and breathed in deeply. Blue Zen, ginger, flower essences, and peppermint oil all tempted me with their luxurious fragrances, but I quickly settled on the blue Zen. I'm drawn to it each time. I love it. I opened my eyes and said, "That one!"

She smiled. "Good choice," she said. "Everyone sees the name 'Stress Reliever' on the other bottle, and they immediately pick that scent whether they like it or not! Drives me crazy. I want them to give all the oils a chance, but I guess we are all so stressed out, we don't even know differently."

I looked at her without thinking much of it and said, "I'm not stressed."

She looked at me quizzically, like I was an alien, like she wasn't sure if she could believe me or not. People who live unstressed? This is a thing?

I have a friend who chooses to give birth to her babies naturally in the comfort of her home. Her last baby was delivered in her bedroom, and the entire pushing process took less than forty-five minutes. Her three other children slept soundly in their own beds and woke up to find baby brother delivered into their world the way most children wake up to find that presents from Santa have magically appeared on Christmas morning. My friend doesn't tell this story out loud too often, because this is a thing? Seriously? People have babies in under an hour in the comfort of their own homes with no medicine? It's about as shocking as the realization that life does not have to be lived in a frenzied, overcommitted fury.

The truth remains: some babies come into the world this way, and some people don't live perpetually stressed-out lives. I have made it my life's mission to be in the latter category, though I will never give birth without an epidural!

The Aveda lady wasn't quite sure what to do with the information that I wasn't stressed, and she immediately asked if I had children. As if children get to determine whether we as adults lead stressful lives. I told her we have a little girl, six years old, and we were doing our best to make sure she wasn't overwhelmed either.

I remember the first time one of Annie's friends told me she was just *so stressed out*. "Really?" I asked her. "What's causing you to feel this way?"

She told me it was her schedule. Soccer one afternoon, gymnastics the next, and swimming on Saturdays. In between that there was all the time spent on the sidelines of her sibling's team sports and in the backseat of the minivan trying to eat dinner and do homework during the car rides.

"Wow, I imagine that is stressful," I told her empathetically.

She answered, "Yeah, I wish I could be like Annie and just play every day."

I remember the concern I had that Annie was missing out or getting behind because she seemed like the only child not yet in dance, sports, or music classes as a four-year-old. Were we limiting her opportunities? I struggled with our decision to just let her come home each day after kindergarten and play. Would she *ever amount to anything?!* The world around us seemed to perpetually whisper in our ears that if we did not immediately enroll her in foreign language lessons and a few extracurricular activities, she would simply be lost in the shuffle and become a truly *average* child.

When her six-year-old friend confessed to me that she was so stressed out, I let out a sigh I didn't realize I'd been holding in. I was relieved to know that by withholding opportunities, I was also withholding a type of stress from Annie that six-year-olds were never meant to carry.

With every opportunity at our fingertips, the vastness screams at us and tells us, "Seize the moment! Run hard with it! Hustle! Opportunity, opportunity, opportunity!" But sometimes opportunity comes at a high cost. And belonging to *all the things* keeps us from truly belonging. I am endeavoring to live a life that does not come at the cost of frenzied fury.

More often than not this is accomplished through intentional un-belonging. Un-belonging myself to the many things I yearn to belong to in order to consciously belong to the few. Somehow I feel like what I am left with is getting closer and closer to the way I felt on that road with my Grandpa.

Birthday Present?

I woke up early on the morning of my thirty-fourth birthday and stared at my phone. I wanted to give myself a present—getting out from underneath my guilt. Scrolling through text messages I hadn't had the time or space to keep up with, I began to text people back with apologies and three-month-late responses. In my hands I held a device that gave me so much opportunity but also sucked my soul away little by little.

What I really wanted to do that morning was write one big email and text message saying something along the lines of, "I love you. I am grateful for you. And I am cheering you on. But I do not currently have the space for the vastness of friendships that have presented themselves to me. I can't keep up. I want to be a good momma, wife, sister, daughter, niece, cousin, neighbor, and friend to the friends that I do everyday life with. Even that is more than I feel capable of." I am learning that unbelonging to the many people I come in contact with is one of the best gifts I can give myself. Who am I to hold the hands of so many? How will I ever hear the crickets and my Grandpa's voice and my Savior's heartbeat if the road I am walking is laced with *all the people*?

When the fear of missing out, the inability to say no, or the misguided belief that you must be everyone's savior causes you to perpetually accept opportunities and friendships you don't have space for, your road will become so crowded that you will find yourself wondering how you belong to everyone but don't belong to anyone. The gnawing loneliness and exhaustion will creep in. You might well wake up on your birthday giving yourself the present of lessening the guilt that has accumulated in not being able to keep up with *all the things* and *all the people*.

I don't ever again want to wake up on my birthday anxious to un-guilt myself. This means that sometimes I must gently untangle and graciously un-belong. Finding our place of belonging often begins with un-belonging ourselves. Being whole isn't always found in belonging to everyone and everything. If I want to heal, grow, wait, pause, listen, linger, and learn, it might well take a concerted effort on my part to slow down and say no. A holy separation from my schedule, responsibilities, even family. A sacred time-out. We must learn to incorporate holy pauses into our day if we are ever to glimpse the healing that hides right beneath our noses.

Finding a Rhythm

I adore the season of fall in Nashville. It's an irrational love because fall is a one-way ticket to winter. And I do not love winter. Not even a little bit. I could be wrong about this, but I think I could go the rest of my life without seeing a single snowflake and be completely content. I despise being cold. I feel it all the way down in my bones, and they chastise me for not living below the equator. It doesn't matter how many layers of clothes I add; my bones are cold and I am miserable.

My mom says if any child were ever destined to live in a nudist colony, it would have been me. In general, I can't get my clothes off fast enough. My rolling around town looking like a giant marshmallow layered in winter coats stands in stark contrast to a girl who would prefer to wear her bathing suit on the beach each day. Winter should look like Miami. Soft breezes, temperatures in the mid- to upper sixties, a light jacket, and a brisk walk by the ocean. That is my idea of December perfection. But I live in Nashville. Winter darkness settles in over the city by 5:00 p.m., it snows, and there are ice storms. The nearest ocean is six hours away.

But I fly through fall as if there is no impending winter. I plow through pumpkin farms, leaf-covered sidewalks, Halloween, football, friends, comfort foods, and a crazy schedule with reckless joy and holiday abandon. And then I wake up on a cold, bleak morning to realize winter has found me. I am irritable and grouchy. Never mind Christmas is on the way. I've got the cold bones. Does anything else really matter? Maybe winter hits hard because fall felt frenzied. If I am not careful, fall can become one long dog and pony show of excitement and exhaustion. All things are full steam ahead. And suddenly what has been a rather mundane and ordinary life begins to hint at the impending arrival of *all* the important things, *all* at once. It's the night before Christmas, and I wonder how I have happened upon it.

Sometimes a year plays out this way: I swear I did something beneficial with my life during the summer. I am just not sure what. I make desperate, begging promises to God that if He will deliver me back to the promised land of spring sunshine, I will be a different woman, a contributing member of society! I fly through fall and find myself at the foot of the manger, a frenzied mess. Don't ask me what happens next. I don't thaw out until April, and everything in between is a lost cause because of the cold bones. Then all the things happen in the spring. Birthdays. Easter. Field trips. Work projects. I try to regain control of it all during Lent, but giving up sugar without giving up control rarely helps anything. I roll back to the summer where I shall do something of worth—just after I rest for a bit on the beach. I get up from the ocean, shake the sand off my feet, and find fall waiting at my doorstep with a pumpkin to boot. Years can tumble by like this if we are not careful.

A year lived without intention or direction is like walking in circles only to end up where you started. Of course beauty can be found on every aimless path, but there is more beauty to behold than the same roads leading back to the same places.

There have been years I have circled the mountain a time or two. With no intentions, resolutions, or direction set, I've happily wandered the same circles and ended up in the very place I started. Some years are like that. But I hope by the end of my life, I won't look back and see mountain ranges, beautiful valleys, and gorges marked by lazy riverbeds that I've missed because I kept my head down and wandered the same tired circle over and over again. I want to live with intention and direction.

Our healing journeys can follow the same patterns. Heads down, frantically and habitually following the same paths over and over again. We can finish a year the way we started, perhaps no worse but certainly no better. We intend on making progress in our healing journeys, but we are sidetracked by sunshine, stalled out by schedules, and driven by distractions. Then one day we wake up in the coldest season, surprised by all the broken things wrapped up in one big, shiny box sitting under the Christmas tree waiting for us. Nothing says "Merry Christmas" like "here's all your crazy you haven't dealt with yet." How have we arrived here? How have we journeyed through an entire year with such little progress in our healing journeys? The answer is simple. We have been sidetracked from doing the hard work of healing by diverting ourselves into everything else. It is the enemy's most successfully utilized tool—distraction from intention.

If it is your intention to be made well, you must put in the hard work of healing long before the next disaster strikes or winter creeps in. Healing cannot be fully achieved if we only seek it during triage. And it can't happen with our heads down as we follow the same paths by memory. Without a clear plan in place to be rooted in a healing journey, our lives will wildly wane with the ebb and flow of seasons and circumstances. The way one flops about from summer to fall to winter and wonders how Christmas arrived, unexpectedly, on their doorstep says a lot about the rhythm of a life. An unguarded rhythm with no intention leads to the kind of life that jumps from crisis to crisis, holiday to holiday, momentous occasion to momentous occasion. And with this type of living it is very possible to miss healing altogether, because we mark our days by the next major event on the calendar and shuffle through all the others, careless and chaotic. Never taking intentional steps toward healing.

Ordinary Time

Most of life feels like ordinary time, like the long stretch in the liturgical church's calendar where nothing of earth-shattering significance happens after Pentecost and before Advent. Over thirty weeks of nothingness! It is not birth or death but the long, in-between roads of waiting and preparation that lead us there. Ordinary time can feel so mundane and predictable that we begin to believe it is the sum of our existence. Many of us sense the urge to compulsively fill the empty spots on the calendar, while others prefer to waste them away. If we aren't careful, we can get lost in the nothingness of ordinary time and scurry through these off-seasons with little intention or too many distractions.

But if we are mindful in this season and turn our attention in part to the hard work of healing, then these are the very days where we can begin to lay the groundwork for wholeness taking root in our lives. The days when we practice communion with Christ, confession, and living with holy awareness as we seek to observe the healing gifts around us. The days when we do the practical things like connecting to the people in our community, building relationships with our soul nurses, and assembling the right medical team to care for our minds and bodies. We practice the art of untangling, un-belonging, and pacing ourselves. We become people of prayer who sink deeper into our faith and ask God to keep us mindful of His love and presence. We uncover the parts of our past that need to be set free . . . and we set them free. We move into our healing day by day, simply and unadorned.

"I've been wondering if, underneath that fear of time, I was longing for someone to tell me that ordinary is good," author Micha Boyett says. "Can I believe that God loves the ordinary?"[2]

God loves ordinary. Ordinary time is the season in which the balm of healing takes root in the broken. Neither dying, grieving death, anticipating life, or giving birth to what is new, ordinary time is the season in which all people can settle onto a level ground where daily healing rhythms can be discovered and practiced. Ordinary time is not so ordinary after all.

16

Receiving Gifts

Rolling plains spread out as far as the eye could see until they disappeared into the jagged dark folds of the black mountains. Lightning struck the ground, seemingly a hundred miles away, and the clouds swirled with colors I had never seen.

The man behind the rental car counter tried to grab my attention. "Ma'am? First time here in South Dakota?"

I nodded mindlessly, staring out the floor-to-ceiling windows behind him. "It's better than I imagined. My Grandpa grew up in Kennebec." I was bewitched by the ferocious green grass and wind-whipped hills unfolding like gentle waves right behind the glass and swaying on into South Dakota forever.

"Grain farmer?" he asked as he continued to process my reservation. "Was your grandpa a grain farmer?"

"No. His dad was a grain farmer. Grandpa was third-generation German and played farm league for the Red Sox. Then he became a brilliant electronics mathematician and joined the Air Force."

"Oh, nice. So, do you want hail insurance? We recommend hail insurance."

I shook my head no. Back in my twenties when I traveled with my husband and our band, he always took care of the rental car people because he knew my resolve was weak; they talked me into every kind of insurance and upgrade they were allowed to offer. It's one of my worst traits. If you are nice, you can talk me into buying anything. This is why I am not allowed to open the front door when some cute kid shows up with their cookie brochure or a European exchange student comes peddling magazines. This is why I am absolutely barred from going to craft fairs where sweet little old men sit whittling pieces of wood to sell in order to take care of their dear, dying wives. Of course, there is a good chance their wives *aren't* dying and they just enjoy wood whittling. But it's too late. I've already crafted the narrative in my heart—I will buy all their wood.

Ryan spends half our marriage reminding me that I cannot buy things we don't need or want simply because the people selling them are *sweet*. This is hard for me. If you are nice, I will buy your music, art, crafts, cookies, tickets to your spaghetti dinner, encyclopedias, Dead Sea skin care products, essential oils, protein shakes, vacuums, last-a-lifetime knives, and newly butchered cow you claim to be selling out of the back of your truck. I will buy all your things with all the money I don't actually have. And even though I am fully insured behind the wheel of every car I drive, I have been known to cave at the rental car counter too.

Ryan sits me down before each trip to coach me on all the things. "Say no to all the insurances they offer you. *All of them.* You already have insurance. And don't buy the Sirius XM package—you don't even like good music. People who only listen to music from the 1990s shouldn't be allowed to have satellite radio. Get the check from the promoter. Preferably before you go on stage. Do you know which hotel you're staying in? Seriously, Jen, you have to know which hotel you're staying in. You leave in two hours. *You're killing me.*"

As I disappear inside the airport, he yells out the window, "And don't let them talk you into a GPS!"

That's usually how the coaching goes. I wonder how I travel and arrive back home alive without this man. It is nothing short of a miracle.

"So, ma'am, you *don't* want hail insurance? Because we *highly* recommend it. South Dakota is known for its hailstorms this time of year."

I gave him my most resolute no. *Hail, no!* I am standing strong against your sweet Dakota offers. I will not cave. Hail in South Dakota? Who's ever heard of such a thing! Then again, who's heard much about South Dakota? You know it's on the map and somebody somewhere knows something about it. You just don't know any of those people. There is a big mountain with dead presidents on it, and they have black hills, grain farmers, and a sister state. That's about all I've got on the place. So I clearly have enough information to deduce an intelligent hypothesis on whether or not they are plagued by hailstorms. Who would have ever guessed South Dakotans fought hailstorms?

But apparently they do. Because one day later while my rental car sat in an uncovered parking lot and I sat backstage at the Hills Alive Music Festival, I watched those hills come straight to life.

The wind came first. Howling and growling and hurling things right off stage. Swirling black clouds like enormous dinosaurs stomping their way across the sky followed close behind. It only took a matter of moments for the dark to sweep in and replace the light. Then the heavens opened up and hail came pouring down. I ran for cover backstage and sat in an RV set up as a greenroom for artists and watched the biggest balls of ice I've ever seen in my life falling from the sky. There were two other bands crammed into the RV, and we pressed our noses against the windows, watching in awe as the sound engineers, light crews, and stage techs were pelted by flying objects while they frantically tried to salvage the equipment.

Ma'am, you don't want hail insurance? Because we highly *recommend it.*

The rental car man's voice echoed in my ears. My eyes welled up with tears. Why in the world didn't I listen to him? Why didn't I trust my gut? I saw those swirly dark clouds hours ago; I should've known they would produce marching orders for disastrous dinosaurs that would conquer the prehistoric land with their mighty stomps. Another ten minutes and they had marched themselves clear on over to the sister state. The sun was shining like nothing had happened, and the crews began to clean off the stage while soaking-wet festival goers reveled in the muddy memories of music life. My tears turned to frustration. Plane tickets to South Dakota were expensive, and I already wasn't breaking even on this trip. The last thing I needed was hail damage to my rental car. And with the severity of that downpour, it wasn't a matter of *if* the car was damaged, it was a matter of *how badly.*

I still had plenty of time before my set, and since the festival grounds shared a parking lot with the hotel where artists were staying, I decided to go ahead and get it over with and see how much damage the car had amassed. Each step was mixed with anxious thoughts, futile prayers to undo history, and frustration at myself for not getting hail insurance.

It was as bad as I had suspected. Like a thousand golf balls had been hurled from space by angry dinosaurs kind of bad. I walked circles around the tiny black Kia covered in craters and cried hot, angry tears. I decided to move the car closer to the backstage area. For what reason, I have no idea. Just in case the heavens opened up again and I needed to throw my body onto the car as a human shield?

Looking back, I often wonder if it was the prompting of the Holy Spirit that put the thought into my mind. A holy suggestion. Maybe there are millions of holy suggestions floating around waiting for us to become aware, waiting for us to listen and act.

There were no parking spots close to the backstage area, so I created my own. This is completely legal when you are emotionally distraught. As soon as I parked the car in my created parking spot, I saw a woman staring at me. She was older and weathered, taking a long drag off her cigarette and watching me.

Great, I thought. *Security.* I acted like she wasn't looking at me and avoided eye contact. If she were working the back parking lot and needed me to move my car, she would have to come ask me. I wasn't offering myself up, that's for sure. But I had to walk past her in order to get back into the venue, and as I did, she began walking purposefully toward me. I felt a familiar fear creeping in, the one I've carried since I was a young girl, which leaves me feeling panicked when someone older than me is about to discipline me. I hate getting in trouble; my heart quickens every single time.

She continued walking resolutely toward me, and I stared harder at the concrete below my feet.

"Excuse me, miss." Her voice, raspy, hung in the crisp air.

"I'm sorry. I know I'm not supposed to be parked here. I'll move it."

"Oh, no, I don't work here, sweetie. Just thought I recognized you. Are you the girl who sings that 'Hope Now' song? That song has meant so much to me and some people real close to me."

Because I was expecting the worse, this conversation of grace made me laugh for a moment and brought tears to my eyes before I even had a chance to blink them back. Big, dramatic, uninvited tears came because of her surprising words. I tried to apologize for them.

"I'm sorry. Just feeling a bit emotional. Yes, ma'am. I'm that girl."

"Are you okay? Can I do anything for you?"

"I'm okay," I said, shaking my head in disagreement at what I was saying, laughing at myself, and wiping the tears away. "It's just, I rented a car for this trip and the guy asked if I wanted hail insurance and I didn't get it. Because who knew South Dakota had hailstorms, you know? And the car got hit bad. I've been stressed-out about money lately and can't believe I didn't get the stupid hail insurance. That's it. I'm okay, though." I smiled at my own drama.

She dropped her cigarette butt and put it out with the heel of her worn cowgirl boot. Every wrinkle on her face told a story. She was slender and a head taller than me. Her eyes were wild and alive, her smile tough and tender. All at once I felt like she might give me a hug and accidentally smother me at the same time. I loved her and was afraid of her, and I didn't know the first thing about her. Not even her name.

She looked deep into my eyes like she was an angel. "Well, you came here for heaven, not hail," she said matter-of-factly. "Let me take care of this. Can you come with me for a minute?"

It all happened so quickly. The security guard turned parking lot angel led me through rows of cars until we arrived at a big red truck. She climbed two silver steps and disappeared into the front of the cab, rummaging through things. And when she emerged, her hands were full of money. She counted out one thousand dollars in cash, placed it in my hands, and looked deep into my eyes again.

"Thank you for your music and for giving us hope. When you think of South Dakota, you think about how you came to give people a taste of heaven, not hail." She winked at me and smiled that tough, tender smile. And I couldn't even cry. I had no idea how to process what had just happened.

We walked back to the festival side by side, learning bits of one another's stories. She didn't like people to know she smoked, so she always snuck out back. I didn't like getting in trouble, so I'd tried to avoid her. "You'd make a great security guard!" I said playfully. She and her husband were farmers and had just sold their land. Maintaining that kind of land was too much, but boy, was she going to miss it. Just about that time we ran into her husband and she filled him in on our encounter, explaining why my hands were full, holding *their* money.

"Well, did you give her enough? Not just for the car, did you give her what she needs to help her keep doing her ministry?" he asked.

My jaw fell wide open. Who were these people? And how in the world did a cigarette break and a hailstorm lead to this? Gifts come from the most unexpected places.

Two hours later I was in their motel lobby (yes, a motel—they wouldn't hear of staying in the frilly, expensive places) meeting the friends and family who had traveled with them to the festival. They wanted to give me enough money to cover the cost of my ministry travel for the rest of the summer. This equaled thousands of dollars. They handed me a check and treated me like I was their long-lost granddaughter.

I watched with an out-of-body feeling, as if I were in a movie. And finally the tears came. Who was I to know such generosity and love? How do you respond to a gift of that magnitude?

An hour later, once our motel laughter and conversation ended, I called Ryan and told him what had happened. His responses were typical.

"You can't take that kind of money from strangers, Jen."

As if I asked for the money! As if it were somehow corrupt since it was coming straight from the hands of unknown strangers and all.

"What do they want in return?"

As if all gifts come with stipulations, bribes, and expectations. This for that.

"Are you sure?"

As if you can be sure about such things. No. I'm not sure. But what does one do when she is handed a check from a stranger for a lot of money? Say, "I'm just not sure about this yet"?

And finally, the response I was waiting for.

"Wow."

We both sat on the phone muttering our "wows" and feeling especially awed and grateful.

If we are to be made well, we must learn how to accept gifts. Gifts from strangers and gifts from acquaintances. Gifts from perceived enemies and gifts from friends and family. The self-reliant, independent, prideful ego will rear its head and say absolutely not! The Western soul has been conditioned to fix itself. Self-reliance is regarded as a premium character trait. We do not know how to open our hands well and receive the gifts of others.

This becomes rooted and developed at a young age. We have raised an entire generation of children who don't open birthday presents in front of their peers. There are many reasons why this may have become a common practice. It's not polite; it may incite jealousy; we want the focus to be on the friendships and not the gifts; there is a chance one child brought a nicer gift than another; we don't want children to experience comparison or shame; and we are unsure if our own children will respond with enough excitement and gratitude. But perhaps at the heart of the movement is the notion that we have forgotten how to graciously accept gifts. How to let love be lavished upon us. In a culture where we expect everyone to earn his or her own way, we must relearn how to receive. We must fight the voice that says we don't deserve it, we haven't earned it, it might come with strings attached, or it could be a con. It's a gift! Mutter "wow" and be in awe.

The best way to practice receiving gifts is by welcoming babies into the world. When a baby arrives we draw in close and stare at the tiny breathing lips and chunky folds of skin, mesmerized that the wrinkly raisin in front of us grew inside another human. What a miracle! It grew arms, legs, a liver, eyebrows, a personality—right smack-dab in the middle of a stomach—and came crying into the world. What a gift! When we stare at babies we know we are staring at something sacred and divine. We are *wowed*. Little-beating-heart gifts.

In the same way that we invite the gift of a baby into the world, we ought to invite gifts into our own lives. One does not assume a tiny baby to be a con, a strings-attached lease, or something that has somehow been earned or deserved. Babies are mysterious miracles that we welcome with deep awe, wonder, and gratitude. Every gift should be welcomed into our lives as such. I learned that in South Dakota.

17

Miracle after Miracle

She was eight years old the first time her dad sold her body to another man at a truck stop. He told her she needed to help support the family and this was her way of contributing her fair share. The abuse went on for over a decade, and when she finally spoke up, her dad went uncharged and she was shunned by her family. With no family, education, or concept of what a normal life might be like, she did the only thing she ever knew how to do—sold her body. She was in her late twenties, hoping to find work one night, when God spoke to her and our paths divinely intersected.

Typically she worked outside of arena events because men, amped up from games and gambling, were more likely to buy her service on their way out. It was an exceptionally cold night when a middle-aged woman approached her and asked if she wanted a ticket to the show happening inside the arena.

"No," she responded.

The woman insisted, "It's cold out here—you should go inside and warm up."

She responded matter-of-factly, "This is where I work."

The woman thought for a minute and held out her hand, offering up the ticket. "Well, it's a Christian concert, so you may not be getting much work tonight. Keep it just in case."

She took the ticket and shoved it in her pocket. At the height of winter, Minneapolis can break the most seasoned Minnesotan. Eventually she went inside the building to warm up.

Sometimes the Holy Spirit lays something heavy on our hearts, and we act upon it but never see the outcome. They are usually quiet, small acts of kindness and faithfulness that go largely unnoticed in a fast-paced, Instagram-worthy world. But they matter. Following through on the tiny promptings bouncing around in your heart often changes the course of someone else's day. In some cases it changes their life. If only we have the space, courage, gumption, selflessness, and time to act upon what we hear, we might be a part of making another person well.

I often wonder about the lady who had the nerve to listen to the Holy Spirit and hand a prostitute her extra ticket to a Christian concert. If only she knew how that one act changed this girl's life. If only she knew the end of the story. One day she will. We will sit with our Savior and a recounting will be made. God will tell her the end of this story. I hope I'm there to witness that moment. God Himself will reward the quiet faithfulness of His children.

Alabama

Four years later the girl from Minneapolis, who took the concert ticket and eventually went inside the arena to warm up, wound up at a safe house for sexually trafficked women in the middle of Alabama. She was ready for a new life but unsure of what that might look like. Was it even possible? Would anyone give her a job? She would work hard and get her GED, but how would she get work without any references? Her past haunted her. Could she forgive herself? Did God forgive girls who gave their bodies away? She wrestled with pain unimaginable and remembered all the things she wanted to forget.

When she arrived in Alabama weeks before Christmas, her heart was heavy and her spirit discouraged. The night I met her, she sat behind a fancy place setting in the modest Baptist church, feeling as though her life was too far gone.

The small-town Baptist church has a long tradition of loving on women in need. Throughout the year they pour into women's shelters across the metropolitan city next door, and then at Christmas they invite the abused, addicted, and homeless ladies down to their suburb for a special feast and holiday concert. Women from the church host a table for women from the shelters. They decorate the tables, line them with decadent desserts, and act as hostesses throughout the night, making sure their guests feel at home and loved on. Men from the church dress up in three-piece suits and serve as waiters.

After dinner is cleared away, the men come back in the room with brand-new purses hanging off their arms. (Think Oprah Christmas when the elves come through the studio, with fun music playing and sparkly new gifts piled in their arms.) The purses are big and colorful and filled with toiletries and new Bibles. The room is full of clapping and the murmur of excited women.

Before leaving the banquet hall and going next door to the sanctuary for the Christmas program, the women are given a card to fill out. It says something along the lines of, "Do you have any questions for us about God?"

The girl from Minneapolis picked up her pen and wrote her question. "Does God even see me or want me?"

She left the card on the table and headed to the sanctuary.

We Are All Broken

Sometimes I panic before I open my mouth to sing and speak. What if what I have is not enough? Each new group in each new city is different. Many times I sit in the back of the room as people walk in, and I pray over them and the words I am about to speak and sing. I'm suddenly struck with the fact that even though the event at hand is of utmost importance to me, I am simply a speck on people's journey. This is incredibly humbling. I have their attention for sixty minutes. That's it. Then they go back to living their lives. My job in those brief moments (as I see it) is to introduce myself, gain the trust of the audience, entertain, encourage, and leave them with some measure of hope and beauty, which perhaps invites them to open their eyes and see God's presence in the world around them. *No pressure.*

The only time I am nervous on stage is when I realize the weight of that responsibility while simultaneously realizing that not a *single* person in the room seems to be tracking with me. I immediately feel small. And scared to death. And my armpits get embarrassingly sweaty.

I sat on the stage in Alabama and nervously watched the women walk in. I felt intimidated—they had lived a lot more life than me. They walked in the room with their stories on their sleeves, and I was afraid they wouldn't welcome me. *What if you have nothing to offer them? What if they just think you're a happy, privileged girl they can't relate to?* The voice whispered its lies.

I hate *the voice.* When I reach the end of my life, I will have told the voice to shut up more times than I care to remember. It never seems to go away, though it is easier to distinguish now and is banished as soon as it rears its ugly head. I speak the words of Scripture out loud, the words that echo my belovedness, and silence the critic. If we are to be made well, we must learn how to silence the voice that seeks to tear us down with the voice of truth.

I sang the first song to the audience of women, and they seemed to stare through me blankly. I was from Mars, they were from Venus—we weren't connecting. So as my musicians began to play the introduction to the next song, I decided to alter the set and tell the women a bit of my own story. How a few years ago I was pregnant and leaving on tour when my husband and I discovered that our band's sixteen-passenger van and trailer and all the musical gear and equipment we used to make a living had been stolen from our apartment parking lot. I told them about how the van was stolen a second time from a *different* parking lot three months later. How we replaced everything with insurance money and then were promptly in a head-on collision with a tree that had fallen in the middle of the road during a storm. How by the end of that year, we couldn't find an insurance company that would insure us, but we had to honor the contracts for shows, so we rented an RV from a private owner and hit the road. I told them how the RV broke down the first four days and then there was an explosion, and it burned to the ground and we lost much of what we owned.

I told the ladies what it felt like to encounter so much loss in a year and how it led to the breakup of the band, near bankruptcy for my husband and me, and the overwhelming lostness that ensued as I tried to figure out what to do next with my life. The few things I knew I had in common with these women are that we had each experienced not-how-I-planned-it moments in our lives, and we longed for someone to give us hope as we stared into the blank, unknown future.

"Our brokenness isn't the same, but we are all broken in our own ways," I told them. My words were flowing as if they were not my own but the Holy Spirit's Himself. "The hope of Christmas is that in the broken, Emmanuel is near. Healing us. Making us well. He knows the way forward in the dark. He knows how to set us free. He sees us."

I felt strongly that I should change the order of songs and asked one of the musicians to switch the set. Then I began to sing the band's most well-known song, "Hope Now." And that's when I noticed the girl from Minneapolis weeping.

He's Got My Attention

At the end of the night she waited by the back table to tell me her story.

She had never heard about a loving God and certainly had not heard Christian music. But one night, four years prior, she was working outside an arena in Minneapolis when she was given a ticket to go inside. It was particularly cold that night, and she wouldn't have gone in except she needed to warm up. As she walked in the building the lights were just going down, and a very pregnant girl waddled on stage and sang a song that moved her to tears. A song had never made her feel that way before, but it captured her, and for the first time in a long time she felt as though hope were somehow possible for her. She left after one song.

Some weeks later as she got in the car to take a job, the buyer put his hand on her leg and instructed her to turn on the music. She turned the radio on and that very song was the first one she heard. Time and time again the song found her, and God whispered something deep inside her she had not heard before—that she wasn't alone and hope could be found in the most hopeless of places. She was reaching a turning point.

Now four years later she found herself in this tiny church thousands of miles away, feeling used up, hopeless, and heavy. Starting over was hard, and new life didn't happen right away. It was requiring the kind of work that felt never ending and exhausting, and she was beginning to wonder if she would ever truly be able to have a second chance. She wondered if God even knew her name and her story. If God even cared.

And that's when I sang the song she heard me sing all those years ago when she had been given a free ticket and came in off the streets to warm up. As I sang "Hope Now" at the beginning of that Christmas concert in Alabama, she wept as she realized I was the same girl who had sung "Hope Now" over her in Minnesota. God whispered deep in her heart, *I saw you in Minneapolis and I see you right now. I sent her for you both times so that you would know I am here. I am with you. I have always been. Of course I know your story.*

She wrote me an email later that night and said, "Tonight at the dinner I had written on a prayer card that I wanted to know if God even saw me or wanted me . . . and then I walked in and saw you. God has my attention. I will never be the same."

Several months after that she reached out to let me know she was being baptized. I responded with the following letter:

Hi, Joy,

It is so good to hear from you, and this is the most wonderful news! I am amazed how God just keeps calling us to Him, reminding us of who we truly are, His beloved. I am grateful that you have fallen into His arms and are taking part in such a beautiful sacrament like baptism that symbolizes NEW LIFE. I always thank God for the sweet, sweet miracle story He allowed us to share together in November.

Literally one month after the worst moment in my life— sitting with my sister's two sweet baby girls who had died—I felt such a huge hole. And in that very moment it was like God began to wage a fight for me, on my behalf, that I had never seen before. Miracle after miracle began to unfold. It has reminded me that miracles don't always come the way we think they should, but that doesn't mean they aren't still happening.

Joy, meeting you was one of my miracles. That God would lead two girls from Minneapolis, Minnesota, to the middle-of-nowhere Alabama when we both needed to know His hand was holding us will never stop amazing me. Ending up in the same place at the same time twice? I would say, "What are the odds?" but it's beyond odds. It's a story of a God who saw you then and sees you today and whispers, "I know you, Joy; I am for you, am with you, and have fought for you."

And that same God says to me, "I see you, Jenny. I am working on your behalf. I have been with you and will be with you; I am weaving together a story too redemptive for you to fully comprehend." I will always be grateful for this.

Much Love,
Jenny

Her response will always be with me.

My baptism will be on Tuesday, March 17. Wow, do you know what I just realized? March 17 was the date I first saw you in concert all those years ago. Again, what are the chances? That all these years later, that same day is when I would be getting baptized. I think it's a neat reminder of God's plan and everything.

Thank you so much for your kind words and encouragement. The thought of being able to encourage you—me, a sex trafficking survivor—just has to be God.

I remember that night I wanted to come talk to you so bad, but I was so afraid to say, "Hi, my name is Joy, and I was a prostitute." It isn't really the best way to make friends and influence people, but not once did I see any look of judgment or disgust in your eyes. When I told you, all I saw was love. You still touched me, hugged me, and wanted to talk to me. I wasn't dirty or gross; I was a human in that moment, and it meant the world to me to talk to you.

I literally told anyone who would listen for weeks afterward. The whole thing played a huge part in me really surrendering my life to God. It was like in that moment God loved me through you. I have never experienced anything like it.

I have never experienced anything like it either. Madeleine L'Engle once said, "The only God who seems to me to be worth believing in is impossible for mortal man to understand, and therefore he teaches us through this impossible."[1] It seems to me that God is always at work showing me glimpses of Himself through the impossible. Life doesn't always include the miracles I pray for, but even so, it is chock-full of miracle after miracle after miracle.

In the End

*I*n the end we are made well in our dying. As the body ages, the disease ravages, and the mind diminishes, the soul begins to long for that place where we find our complete restoration. We long for Abba. Perhaps our final sickness is homesickness.

The opening line in a blessing titled *For Death*, written by poet-theologian John O'Donahue, says, "From the moment you were born, your death has walked beside you."[1] I understand this well.

Death has been quietly walking beside me since I was a little girl. My early childhood was relatively free from the darkness of death, and yet I sensed it so near. I was keenly aware that at any moment, I could stop breathing. Anyone could. But this terrifyingly wild thought, once calmed down and detached from emotion, instinctively brought me a sense of freedom. If death was inevitable, walking beside me like a close friend, I was free to live openhandedly—not holding on, grabby and clinging, but dancing, knowing each breath was a gift. O'Donahue's blessing over those who have ears to listen is this: the silent presence of your death would call your life to attention. I've been living at attention for a few decades now.

I had a profound experience at a recent Sufjan Stevens concert when his band began to play the song "Fourth of July" off the album *Carrie & Lowell*—an album centered entirely on the experience of death and dying. The very simple chorus that resounds throughout the entire song says, "We're all gonna die." At the height of the chorus, the band's music began to swell and veer off course from the recording. Lights flashed purple and strobed through the dark Ryman Auditorium. Every musician on stage began to sing, their voices layered on top of one another, "We're all gonna die," over and over and over again. The crowd began to sing along too. A few thousand voices strong singing, "We're all gonna die."

It struck me that we were in an old church converted into Nashville's premier music venue—and it *felt* like church. In that moment the confession of our impending death did not feel fatalistic or pessimistic. It felt holy. Holy to confess our limitations and smallness. Holy to confess that this was not the end of the story. Holy to acknowledge there was hope in the living *and* hope in the dying.

I was recently asked to pray for a miracle for a young mother on her deathbed. She fought for so long to beat the cancer that invaded her body and dreamed of living long enough to watch her baby girl take her first step.

The cancer had gone away and everyone celebrated. But months later it came back swift and fierce. Seven short weeks after the revelation, hospice was called in. It was a matter of days, they said. Two, maybe three. She fell into a deep sleep, and her heart rate soared at 170 beats per minute for days on end. But she kept fighting—not wanting to let go yet. A body may be ready to die, but sometimes a heart and soul just aren't. She fought on.

People around the world were enlisted to pray for a miraculous healing. But as I prayed for a miracle, I sensed it was time to start praying for her transition, for her ability to let go and make the journey to the other side. So I prayed for the miracle of death.

"When I am lying down to die, I want someone to recite the prayer in the *Book of Common Prayer* that says, 'Go forth faithful servant,' put some lavender oil on me, and then feel like they helped me heal," Becca Stevens says. "If I thought someone at my deathbed was praying for me to stand up and walk, I would hope someone else close by would invite that person into silence to remember that there is healing in death."[2] Sometimes our desperate prayers for earthly healing keep us from embracing the beautiful gift we have been given to walk one another to the Healer for our final healing. In the tension of life and death—living and leaving—it's hard to know what to ask God for in those moments.

One of the earliest songs I wrote was called "Hold On, Let Go," and it depicted the struggle I felt as I prayed for my Papaw, who was dying of aggressive brain cancer. He meant the world to me, and in the face of his illness I didn't know what to pray for. The miracle of life or the miracle of death. At the time, I felt as though I had to choose. Now I am comfortable asking for both.

To pray for miracles and the ability to let go in the same breath doesn't cheapen our faith; it acknowledges our human condition. "Is it proper to grieve and rejoice simultaneously?" Madeleine L'Engle asks. "If the love I define in my own heart as Christian love means anything at all; yes. If the birth of Christ as Jesus of Nazareth means anything at all; yes."[3]

We're all going to die, and there is a time that the healing miracle becomes being made whole in the presence of Jesus. As we pray for the miracle of death, we are really praying for resurrection. We are praying for wholeness. The art of dying well has been taught to us by many beautiful souls like Roger Ebert, Kara Tippetts, professors Randy Pausch and Morrie Schwartz, Joey Feek, and the many other sons and daughters, grandmas and grandpas, moms and dads, and little children who take our hands, tell us to breathe deep and be brave, and teach us through their dying what it looks like to truly be made well. Morrie Schwartz said it best in the book *Tuesdays with Morrie*, which chronicles his death: "The truth is, once you learn how to die, you learn how to live."[4]

Resurrection

My friend's husband left her three years ago, and she still cries each morning. She lies in bed before she wakes up her babies and goes to the job she never planned on working to pay the bills—and she prays. Some mornings she thinks, *This is the day I will die.* The day she just can't do it anymore. Can't keep her head above water, can't fight back the sadness, can't be a single momma to three, living a life she never imagined. But each time she thinks she can't take another step or bear the pain any longer, she says, "Resurrection happens." Sometimes the tears come, she says, because in the midst of this broken place there is so much unexpected goodness and love poured onto her by others and by God Himself that she can hardly handle it. These are the footprints of the King and His kingdom—resurrection.

Resurrection is happening all around us. The body fights its way out of ICU or the marriage is miraculously restored. The

PET scan comes back clean. The apology you never imagined would come, comes. Baby Katherine is born. And I can't even write it without weeping.

Fourteen months after Maggie and Ellen went to be with Jesus, my sister gave birth again. Katherine Eleanor Miller came into the world healthy and whole, early in the morning, at home—the way my sister always dreamed of having her babies. Her birth swept through our hearts and brought light and life the way resurrection always does. Sometimes resurrection comes bold and mighty. We celebrate with songs unending.

But more times than not, it seems resurrection comes in small, almost imperceivable ways. It's a bit unglamorous, if you ask me. All too often healing looks less like cured diseases and more like church ladies showing up at the hospital with silk pajamas. Less like a perfect childhood and more like a really great therapist and a leather journal stained with cathartic tears. Less like being rescued from the sting of death and more like friends showing up during the deathy moments with bread and wine and free babysitting. Songs, sunsets, and strangers—these are the everyday sacred moments that find me and sustain me when I have all but given up. They are enough. Bit by bit I am made well.

Healing looks like disciples gathered around the table, finding life through community. Like jumping off trains, going to concerts, planting a garden, befriending a homeless man, or taking a morning walk through winter woods. It comes in wave after wave of faithful, never-ending mercy. Tiny shoots of grass poking through thawed winter ground. A kind word reviving a weary heart. Food arriving, laundry disappearing and coming back clean, a bird perched on your finger, an amazing hospital chaplain, a helpful human on the other end of the medical bills phone call, a letter in the mail, a stranger buying your coffee, the beauty in your grandchild's eyes, watching the sunset and knowing you are loved—realizing your heart is still faithfully beating.

"Can you breathe here? Here where the force is greatest and only the strength of your neck holds the river out of your face?" Annie Dillard asks. "Yes, you can breathe even here. You could learn to live like this. And you can, if you concentrate, even look out at the peaceful far bank where maples grow straight and their leaves lean down."[5] Even when the water feels like it is rushing over our faces, if our eyes and heart remain open we will see life coming from death. We can breathe here.

This is the road to becoming—our journey of being made well. We are living in between the now and the not yet. It is the story of Adam and Eve and Advent and Easter and every moment in between—the great story of rescue.

So often in our desperation to prolong life on earth, we forget that complete restoration can never fully happen here. Healing in this life is but a foretaste of what is to come. Now we live in the shadow of resurrection. But one day the clouds will roll back and there will no longer be the shadow of resurrection—there *will be* resurrection. We know it now in part, but soon we will know it full well. No longer catching small glimpses of being made well. *All* will be well. As it was in the beginning. The journey doesn't end this side of heaven. The miracle of wholeness is still on its way. When the divine intersects with us on the other side of earth living, we will finally be made well.

Until then we are invited to be made well around dinner tables, in doctors' offices, and at the dog park. Healed through restored relationships and rest. Wooed into a journey that leads to wholeness whether our physical bodies are cured or not.

Beckoned to meet Jesus in the ebb and flow of real life and be healed through His incarnational presence at the crossroads. Our job is to remember that God is divinely showing up in the midst of our deathy, *holey* lives. To live with eyes open, to remember that healing happens around each new corner—this is the work at hand.

Where do heaven and earth intersect? Where does the temporal meet the eternal? When will the Divine show up and faithfully, generously heal in the midst of our deathy, uncured lives? You need only remember the beating of your own heart to know that healing is already at work and miracles are at hand. Resurrection is happening all around us. Healing happens here and now.

"Do you want to be made well?" Jesus asks.

The invitation stands.

Many Thanks

To Sarah, Ray, Abigail, Maggie, Ellen, and Katherine—you have shown the world a gut-wrenching and beautiful picture of love, constancy, and redemption. No truer picture of Emmanuel has been seen than in your story. Thank you for letting me share your journey and, in so doing, offer hope and healing to many.

To Mom, Dad, Melissa, Tim, Lexie, Clara, and the entire Miller clan—you are the best family a girl could ask for. We have walked through unspeakable pain together and still found a way to laugh and sing. Thank you for showing up on that one Thanksgiving. And for every day before and after. I love learning how to be made well alongside you.

To the most faithful friends and family—you have walked with me, carried me, and brought wine, laughter, tears, and silence along the way. Thank you—the whole army of you.

To Kristin, Lindsay, and Jude—you are loved and you are forgiven. I am grateful for your voices cheering me on while I trudged through the hardest hours of writing this book.

To those who have invited me into your story—thank you for trusting me with your sacred journeys. They are so often laced with heartache and pain, and I carry that with you. But then? Resurrection. Thank you for letting me glimpse God's grace in your stories.

To Jana Burson and Rebekah Guzman, editors extraordinaire—you ladies make things beautiful. I am so grateful to have your fingerprints on my books.

To Don Gates—you have cheered me on for no good reason. Thank you for your incredible belief and support in my words. In this story.

To Sufjan Stevens—we've never met except in my living room each morning as your words guided and shaped my soul while I wrote these words. Thank you for *Carrie & Lowell*. What a gift.

To Annie—every day you teach me more and more about what it means to be free and fully alive. Your beauty spills out from deep inside you and changes everything it touches. I am so proud of you and love you more than you will ever know. You were made well.

To Ryan—somehow you see the best version of me. Of us. Of our little family and this great big world. You see peace, redemption, second chances, beauty, and goodness, and you teach me to look for it. These words exist because you sequester me, push me, inspire me, and know how to rearrange chapters when I can't seem to find the way. Thank you for being on this journey with me.

Notes

In the Beginning

1. Sally Lloyd Jones, *The Jesus Storybook Bible* (Grand Rapids: Zondervan, 2007), 15.

Chapter 2: Half-Baked Miracles

1. Daniel 3:16–17 NLT, emphasis added.

Chapter 3: Beloved

1. James Bryan Smith, *Embracing the Love of God* (New York: HarperOne, 2008), 40.
2. See Matthew 5:14; John 10:14–16; 2 Corinthians 6:18; John 15:15.
3. Rachel Held Evans, *Searching for Sunday* (Nashville: Thomas Nelson), 19.
4. Robert Benson, *Between the Dreaming and the Coming True* (New York: HarperSanFrancisco, 1996), 6.
5. Jones, *Jesus Storybook Bible*, 36.

Chapter 4: Holey, Holey, Holey

1. "Pope Claims Christmas Is a 'Charade' Due to Continued War across the World," *The Telegraph*, November 19, 2015, http://www.telegraph.co.uk/news/worldnews/the-pope/12006485/Pope-claims-Christmas-is-a-charade-due-to-continued-war-across-the-world.html.
2. Ian Maclaren, Ian Maclaren Quotes, https://www.goodreads.com/author/quotes/168031.Ian_Maclaren.
3. Mark 5:9.
4. *Merriam-Webster Online*, s.v. "healthy."
5. Becca Stevens, *Snake Oil* (New York: Jericho Books, 2014), 6.

Chapter 5: Invitations

1. Revelation 3:20.
2. John 5:6 NRSV.
3. Amber Haines, *Wild in the Hollows* (Grand Rapids: Revell, 2015), 181.
4. Jonathan Martin, *Prototype* (Carol Stream, IL: Tyndale, 2013), 5.
5. Smith, *Embracing the Love of God*, 22.

Chapter 7: Healing Hurts

1. Becca Stevens (speech, Grace-St. Luke's Episcopal Church, Memphis, TN, August 29, 2015).
2. See Luke 8:43–47.
3. As always, I am endlessly grateful for Al and Nita Andrews and the work of Porter's Call. Their heart for the artist community as we endeavor to be made well is unparalleled.
4. Stevens, *Snake Oil*, 92–93.

Chapter 8: Slow Dancing

1. Stevens, *Snake Oil*, 30.

Interlude: Sparrows

1. Stevens, *Snake Oil*, 117.
2. Anne Lamott, *Small Victories* (New York: Penguin Books, 2014), 1.
3. Margaret Feinberg, *Wonderstruck* (Brentwood, TN: Worthy, 2012), 52.

Chapter 9: Living with Limps

1. Ryan Gregg, "Hope Now," *Addison Road*, © 2008.
2. Paul Overstreet and Don Schlitz, "When You Say Nothing at All," *Don't Close Your Eyes*, © 1988.

Chapter 11: Emmanuel

1. Stan Mitchell (sermon, Gracepointe Church, Franklin, TN, January 11, 2015).

Chapter 12: Soul Nurses

1. Florence Nightingale Pledge, http://www.nursingworld.org/FlorenceNightingalePledge.
2. Benson, *Between the Dreaming and the Coming True*, 24–25.
3. Barbara Brown Taylor, *An Altar in the World* (New York: HarperOne, 2009), 79.

Chapter 13: Kisses and Confession

1. Smith, *Embracing the Love of God*, 72.

Chapter 15: Sacred Pauses

1. Madeleine L'Engle, *Circle of Quiet* (New York: HarperCollins, 1972), 88.
2. Micha Boyett, *Found* (Brentwood, TN: Worthy, 2014), 70.

Chapter 17: Miracle after Miracle

1. Madeleine L'Engle, *The Irrational Season* (New York: HarperCollins, 1977), 19.

In the End

1. John O'Donahue, *To Bless the Space Between Us* (New York: Doubleday, 2008), 72.
2. Stevens, *Snake Oil*, 88.
3. L'Engle, *Irrational Season*, 24.
4. Mitch Albom, *Tuesdays with Morrie* (New York: Doubleday, 1997), 82.
5. Annie Dillard, *An American Childhood* (New York: Harper & Row, 1987), 150.

About the Author

Jenny Simmons is a dynamic storyteller and lover of people who sees God's redemptive hand at work in the world around her. She is a sought-after musician and speaker who has garnered a devoted following on her blog (www.jennysimmons.com). As the lead singer of the former band Addison Road, Jenny traveled the country performing alongside her husband, Ryan, for over a decade. Jenny and Ryan have been married fourteen years and live in Nashville, Tennessee, with their daughter.

LOVE THE BOOK?

Listen to songs inspired by the stories.

Jenny's albums, *The Becoming* and *To Be Well*, are available exclusively on iTunes and Amazon.

CATCH UP WITH AUTHOR AND SINGER

Jenny Simmons

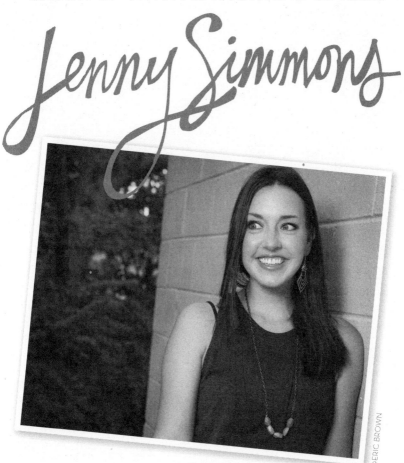

JENNYSIMMONS.COM

f jennysimmonsmusic

🐦 jennysimmons or @jennysimmons

📷 jennysimmonsmusic

LIKE THIS BOOK?

Consider sharing it with others!

- Share or mention the book on your social media platforms. Use the hashtag **#MadeWellBook**.

- Write a book review on your blog or on a retailer site.

- Pick up a copy for friends, family, or strangers—anyone who you think would enjoy and be challenged by its message.

- Share this message on Twitter or Facebook:
  "I loved #MadeWellBook by @JennySimmons @ReadBakerBooks."

- Recommend this book for your church, workplace, book club, or class.

- Follow Baker Books on social media and tell us what you like.

 **Facebook.com/ReadBakerBooks**

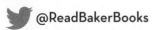 **@ReadBakerBooks**